Foreword by
ROBERT P. MENZIES

Third Wave Pentecostalism in the Philippines:
Understanding Toronto Blessing Revivalism's Signs and Wonders Theology in the Philippines

by

Lora Angeline Embudo Timenia

WIPF & STOCK · Eugene, Oregon

Wipf and Stock Publishers
199 W 8th Ave, Suite 3
Eugene, OR 97401

Third Wave Pentecostalism in the Philippines
Understanding Toronto Blessing Revivalism's Signs and Wonders Theology in the Philippines
By Timenia, Lora Angeline Embudo and Menzies, Robert P.
Copyright © 2020 APTS Press All rights reserved.
Softcover ISBN-13: 978-1-7252-9421-9
Hardcover ISBN-13: 978-1-7252-9422-6
eBook ISBN-13: 978-1-7252-9423-3
Publication date 9/24/2021
Previously published by APTS Press, 2020

Publisher's Preface

We are pleased to offer this seventh title in our APTS Press Monograph Series. This is the publication of the author's Master of Theology thesis done at the Asia Pacific Theological Seminary in Baguio City, Philippines. The purpose of this series is to give our readers broader access to good scholarship that would otherwise be unavailable outside of the academic community. This is part of our ongoing commitment to discipleship through publishing.

The other six titles in this series, *Theology in Context: A Case Study in the Philippines,* by Dave Johnson, *Leave a Legacy: Increasing Missionary Longevity*, by Russ Turney, *Understanding the Iglesia ni Cristo*, by Anne Harper, *A Theology of Hope: Contextual Perspectives in Korean* Pentecostalism, by Sang Yun Lee, *Business In Islam: Contextualizing Mission in Muslim-Majority Nations,* by Robert J. Stefan, and *A Multi-Media Literacy Project: Toward Biblical Literacy in Bangladesh* by Teresa Chai. All are available at www.aptspress.org. If you have any questions, you can reach us through our website. We would be happy to hear from you.

God bless you as you read this book.

THE PUBLISHER

Table of Contents

Publisher's Preface	*iii*
Preface	*vii*
Foreword	*xi*
Dedication	*xv*
Acknowledgments	*xvii*
CHAPTER 1: Introduction	1
CHAPTER 2: Review of Literature on the Toronto Blessing Revivalism	13
CHAPTER 3: Review of Literature on Historical Roots and Theological Antecedents	23
CHAPTER 4: Review of Literature on the Development of the Revivalism in the Philippines	43
CHAPTER 5: Review of Literature on the Filipino Religious System	61
CHAPTER 6: Methodology	81
CHAPTER 7: Presentation of Findings	85
CHAPTER 8: Understanding the Findings	113
CHAPTER 9: Evaluation from a Classical Pentecostal Perspective	129
CHAPTER 10: Evaluating Manifestations	141
CHAPTER 11: Conclusion and Recommendations	153
References Cited	157

Preface

Back in 2013, I was exposed to a revivalist church with a different spirituality from the classical Pentecostal church I grew up in. They espoused that manifestations of gold dust, orbs, angel feathers, miracle money, heavenly gemstones, glory cloud and the like are manifestations of signs and wonders. They called these manifestations as signs of heaven or glory manifestations. Their spirituality was more *revivalistic* and cathartic than mine. Though we shared a common acceptance of the continued miraculous work of the Holy Spirit, their teaching and experience of signs and wonders were different from what I experienced in my classical Pentecostal church.

To clarify, I am from the Assemblies of God in the Philippines. I believe in Spirit-empowerment and the continuation of miracles and signs and wonders. I have often experienced the presence of God in prayer and worship. I speak in tongues and pray for divine healing. I preach the gospel believing that signs and wonders will follow. I am very much a Pentecostal woman. But I have not experienced these "glory manifestations." In fact, meeting people espousing these beliefs surprised and confused me.

Questions began to formulate in my mind about these revivalist churches. I asked myself: "Are these manifestations a form of biblical signs and wonders? Are these manifestations normative and safe for Filipinos, whose innate hyper spirituality often result in forms of folk religiosity?" I also wondered where these revivalist churches came from and how they formulated their theologies. All these questions percolated in my mind for a few years.

By 2015, I began teaching at Bethel Bible College of the Assemblies of God and encountered students who asked the same questions about these revivalist churches. I saw that they too were confused by claims of unusual signs and wonders, and that they wonder about the differences between our classical Pentecostal spirituality and these revivalist churches' spirituality. In an attempt to answer their questions, I browsed books on Pentecostal/Charismatic movement in the Philippines. I asked pastors and teachers about these churches and their teachings. I also began researching about revivalism in the Philippines. What I found out surprised me. There are no books or academic literature about these churches and their theology in the Philippines. It seems that these churches, which started in the late 90s to early 2000 has steadily grown within Filipino Christianity, without academic evaluation or historical explanation. I even asked pastors of these revivalist churches, and they too could not explain when and how their movement began to spread in the country.

With this academic gap in mind, I decided to formally do a field research in an attempt to understand these revivalist churches. I had many questions in mind, but I focused on one main question: What is their theology of signs and wonders in the Filipino perspective? I also asked two sub-questions: What contributed to their historical development in the Philippines, and what are the implications of their theology to Filipino Pentecostal/Charismatics? The research then became my Master of Theology thesis in Asia Pacific Theological Seminary (APTS). Fortunately, my thesis supervisor, Dave Johnson, decided that the work was worth publishing in book form through the APTS Press. This afforded me the opportunity to share my research to a wider audience.

It took some time to complete it, the delay being due to the fact that I was pregnant with my first child at the time of writing. Writing this felt like laboring and giving birth. The end product is the birth of academic literature presenting a historical understanding, a Pentecostal critique and an appreciation of a narrow stream of churches having a revivalist spirituality connected to the Toronto Blessing. Through this, I met few of the most charismatic and God-loving ministers namely, Hiram Pangilinan, Apollo "Paul" Yadao, Miguel Que, and Ronald De Asis Betiwan. They were kind enough to answer questions about their ministries and their theologies. They were humble and open minded enough to be subject to constructive critique from a Filipino classical Pentecostal. They were desirous enough to be heard and understood. I may not totally agree with a few of their theological claims, but I recognize their unique contribution to Pentecostal/Charismatic Christianity in the Philippines and I appreciate their sincere desire for the world to know the glory of Jesus.

I hope that readers of this book recognize that the ultimate motivation of the study is to develop a healthy and academic understanding of this stream of revivalism in the Philippines. It also serves to dispel confusion among classical Pentecostals in the Philippines, and to provide a propositional framework of evaluating manifestations of signs and wonders.

There is still much to be researched and written about Spirit-empowered movements in the Philippines. I hope someday future researchers will embark on a journey of discovery as I did. For now, this book is my small contribution to the unfinished theological task.

Foreword

With this book, Lora Timenia provides the Pentecostal/Charismatic movement with critically-needed tools and wise counsel for evaluating unusual spiritual experiences and phenomena. Her sympathetic yet critical analysis of four influential proponents of the Toronto Blessing revivalism in the Philippines is marked by careful research, informed analysis, and a pastoral heart. Timenia's detailed research and insightful evaluation is communicated in clear language and marked by an irenic spirit. Her ability to instruct and her desire to edify shines through on virtually every page. The result is a book that not only offers valuable counsel for the burgeoning charismatic churches of the Philippines, but one that also provides much-needed pastoral perspective for the global Pentecostal movement.

Timenia's analysis takes full account of the unique cultural and spiritual dynamics that shape the Filipino context. Yet her ability to approach this study from an informed biblical perspective also makes it valuable reading for students, pastors, and church leaders around the world. Additionally, although questions about unusual spiritual phenomena associated with revival meetings are not limited to our contemporary age, the recent emergence of a host of charismatic churches connected to or influenced by the 'Toronto Blessing' revival makes the publication of this book especially timely. Indeed, every generation that has experienced the fresh winds of the Spirit has also needed wise pastoral guidance in order to navigate the resulting storms. Timenia's book provides this kind of guidance for our present generation.

Donald Gee offered sorely needed, godly advice to an earlier generation of Pentecostals. This British Pentecostal statesman was known for his balance, wisdom, and candor. His wise counsel to a young and at times immature Pentecostal church is still worth reading. Gee noted that the more unusual or bizarre forms of behavior that often accompany the coming of the Spirit (shouting, barking, laughing, shaking, etc.) are not in and of themselves "manifestations" of the Spirit. Rather, he noted, these are human responses to the work of the Holy Spirit. The manifestations of the Spirit are, in Gee's view, outlined by Paul in 1 Corinthians 12-14. So, Gee suggested that we should acknowledge these phenomena for what they are: human responses to God's presence. We need not be overly concerned about them, but we certainly should not lift them up as models for all to follow. Rather, the experiences of the apostolic church should serve as our guide. Gee observed that pastoral leadership in these matters is essential; for, while these human responses are relatively common and not intrinsically wrong, they can at times inhibit what God desires to accomplish. When that happens, wise leadership will offer the guidance that is needed to maintain order.[1]

Lora Timenia's fine work will enable a new generation of Christians who are facing a fresh set of questions to offer the wise guidance and pastoral leadership that is so desperately needed today. She too calls us to evaluate our contemporary experiences through the lens of the apostolic church and provides a helpful model for doing so. It is noteworthy that Donald Gee, a European man, provided guidance on this matter for an earlier generation of Pentecostals, while the wise counsel today comes from an Asian woman. This is fitting, for it accurately reflects the nature of contemporary Pentecostalism, which is largely female and predominately located in the Majority World. It also belies the trope that majority world Pentecostals are only interested in experience, not theology or doctrine. This book represents an important contribution to the Pentecostal movement not because it was produced by a Filipina; but rather, because it is an insightful study, steeped in careful research, and rooted in solid theological reflection. I am delighted to warmly recommend this book to any and all Christians who seek to evaluate from a biblical perspective spiritual experiences

---

[1]Donald Gee, *All with One Accord* (Springfield, MO: Gospel Publishing House, 1961), 24-28, 56-59; Gee, *Is it God?* (Springfield, MO: Gospel Publishing House, 1972), passim; Gee, *Concerning Spiritual Gifts* (Springfield, MO: Gospel Publishing House, 1972), 86-101; Gee, *Why Pentecost?* (London: Victory Press, 1944), 37-40.

and phenomena, including contemporary "glory manifestations," and who desire to discern what God is doing in our midst.

Robert Menzies
Easter, 2020

This book is dedicated to

God, for urging me to write this book

and

Karlo, for supporting me throughout the process

Acknowledgments

This study would not have been possible if not for the humility and transparency of four Filipino Neocharismatic ministers, namely, (1) Hiram Pangilinan, (2) Apollo "Paul" Yadao, (3) Miguel Que, and (4) Ronald De Asis Betiwan. These four men willingly accepted the challenge of being interviewed, evaluated, and constructively critiqued in their desire to make known a growing wave of revivalism in the country. I, as the researcher, am deeply grateful for them because of their kindness, openness, and honesty. The primary data they provided and their perspectival explanations have contributed to understanding this movement as part of the Pentecostal/Charismatic movement in the Philippines.

It is not the intent of this book to destructively criticize their revivalist spirituality, but rather, (1) to enlighten readers on the history and theological development of this movement in the country, (2) clearly define their signs and wonders theology, (3) to open an avenue for dialogue between classical Pentecostals and Neocharismatics, and (4) to foster rapprochement. I believe that each tradition has something to offer to the other, and confusion about each other's theologies can be clarified by academic study. I also believe that constructive criticism and openness to correction between co-related movements are necessary for the spiritual health of Filipino Christianity. This is why the study is significant for all those within the Pentecostal/Charismatic movement.

I also would like to extend my heartfelt gratitude to Asia Pacific Theological Seminary who financially undergirded this study. Through this premier institution I finished a Master of Theology in Pentecostal/Charismatic Studies, and this book was a product of that degree. I specifically thank President Yee Tham Wan, Academic Deans Dr. Kay Fountain and Dr. Teresa Chai, Postgraduate Director Dr.

Weldyn Houger, M.Th. Coordinator Dr. Adrian Rosen, and Business Administrators Rev. Kent Parrish and Rev. Ed Benish. All of you contributed to the completion of my studies.

More importantly, I would like to acknowledge the contribution of my thesis supervisor, Dr. Dave Johnson, who journeyed with me throughout this study. His mentorship was priceless, and the learnings I got from him unforgettable. He, being the managing editor of APTS Press, also paved the way for the publication of this research into book form. Thank you also for the editing team he brought in to help make this book reader friendly. Specifically, I thank Jon Smith, the academic editor, for his meticulous editing and for his positivity over my work. I thank also Frank McNelis of the APTS press for his kind assistance in the entire project.

Finally, I thank my family for their unending support. I acknowledge the sponsorship of my parents, Lorna Jane Consuelo B. Embudo and Ranulfo C. Embudo, as well as my sisters Bernadette E. Valencia, Camille Evarose Embudo, and April Lorraine Embudo. I also acknowledge the love and support of my husband Karlo D. Timenia. Without my husband's full backing, this book would not be possible. Thank you everyone.

CHAPTER 1

Introduction

On January 20, 1994, a renewal meeting shook a Toronto-based church (now known as 'Catch the Fire' [CTF]), with holy laughter, visions and trances, miraculous healing, odd physical manifestations, and claims of revitalized spirits.[1] It was dubbed by the British media as the 'Toronto Blessing' (TB), although today its proponents prefer to call it the 'Father's Blessing'.[2] Some believe that the birth of this movement can be traced to John Wimber's Third Wave "theology of power;"[3] while others point to the influence of Pentecostal/Charismatic (P/C) evangelists like Benny Hinn and most notably Rodney Howard-Browne, who was known for a ministry characterized by 'holy laughter' and 'falling under the power'.[4]

However, many Charismatics contend that well before the TB similar revival-like phenomena had been occurring internationally, although some leaders reigned it in.[5] Regardless of its origins, this movement (described by Mark Cartledge as having a revivalist

---

[1] Catch the Fire (CTF) is both a church and a global network led by John and Carol Arnott, which became the launch pad for the Toronto Blessing. Its original name was Toronto Airport Vineyard (TAV) back in 1994, when it was still part of John Wimber's Association of Vineyard Churches (AVC). However, after being ousted by Wimber from the AVC, the church's name was changed in January 1996 to Toronto Airport Christian Fellowship (TACF). Today, it goes by CTF Church in Toronto. In this study, the name Catch the Fire will be used so as to avoid confusion. See Mark Cartledge, "'Catch the Fire': Revivalist Spirituality from Toronto to Beyond," *PentecoStudies* 13, no. 2 (2014): 218, 220.

[2] Margaret Poloma, "Toronto Blessing," in *The New International Dictionary of Pentecostal and Charismatic Movements (TNIDPCM)*, ed. Stanley Burgess and Eduard Van der Maas, revised and expanded. (Grand Rapids, MI: Zondervan, 2003), 1149.

[3] Cartledge, "'Catch the Fire': Revivalist Spirituality from Toronto to Beyond," 218.

[4] Stephen Hunt, "The 'Toronto Blessing': A Rumour of Angels?" *Journal of Contemporary Religion* 10, no. 3 (October 1995), 261.

[5] Ibid., 260.

spirituality⁶) resulted in the development of a stream in the P/C movement that practiced what this study will call a 'Toronto Blessing revivalism'. It also resulted in the spread of a TB revivalist spirituality across the globe, which reached the Philippines through its international network.[7]

The manifestations seen during a revivalist meeting, such as shaking, being slain in the Spirit, weeping loudly, tongues-speaking, seeing visions, and prophesying are not new in the Philippines. Since Pentecostalism entered the country in the late 1920s,[8] physical manifestations like these have been experienced in the fringes of P/C churches. However, the intensity, frequency, and spread of manifestations in TB revivalist meetings are considerably unparalleled.[9]

For instance, in the late 1990s, these revivalists started professing the manifestation of unusual signs and wonders, otherwise known as 'glory manifestations'.[10] In 1999, CTF (then the Toronto Airport Christian Fellowship [TACF]) posted the following official statement on the appearance of 'gold teeth' as a manifestation of signs and wonders in their meetings:

> Why would God fill people's teeth with gold? Perhaps because He loves them and delights in blessing His children. Perhaps it is a sign and a wonder to expose the skepticism still in so many of us. Perhaps His glory and presence are drawing very near.
> On Wednesday evening March 3, 1999, during a TACF Intercession Conference, miracles began happening in people's teeth. By Thursday evening, over 50 people were on the platform testifying to having received what appeared to be gold or bright silver fillings or crowns, which they believed had supernaturally appeared after receiving prayer. Many received

---

[6]Cartledge, "'Catch the Fire': Revivalist Spirituality from Toronto to Beyond," 237.
[7]Ibid.
[8]Wonsuk Ma, "Philippines," *TNIDPCM*, 201.
[9]P. J. Richter, "'God Is Not a Gentleman!': The Sociology of the Toronto Blessing," in *The Toronto Blessing or Is It?*, ed. S.E. Porter and P.J. Richter (London, Darton. UK: Longman and Todd, 1995), 11.
[10] Bill Vincent blogged about a Randy Clark service in October 1998, where people testified to seeing gold dust. John Arnott too reported teeth being filled with gold during his ministry in South Africa. See Bill Vincent, "Gold Dust, Gold Teeth, Gold Flakes. . . " http://www.forgottenword.org/gold-dust.html (accessed January 11, 2019).

two, three, or more (in some cases, up to ten) changed fillings! By Saturday night, there were 198 saying that God had given them a dental miracle; and by Sunday night, well over 300 people testified to this unusual sign. Even now, testimonies continue to pour in.[11]

These 'gold phenomena', together with the manifestation of animal sounds and other esoteric demonstrations, caused many to question the validity of the experience in a TB revivalist meeting.[12]

Regardless of the controversy, some Filipino ministers became recipients of this revivalist spirituality via the internet, media, and literature as well as through the seminars and speaking engagements of visiting revivalists.[13] When Filipino ministers began reading books by John Arnott, Che Ahn, Bill Johnson, Randy Clark, and others, they became open to their revivalist theologies, as well as to their testimonial claims of unusual signs and wonders.[14]

---

[11] The official statement of TACF on gold teeth has been removed from its revamped website; however, a copy of it can be read in the CESNUR webpage. See Toronto Airport Christian Fellowship, "They Go for the Gold: Gold Dust and Gold Teeth Filling Miracles Claimed in Charismatic Churches," *Center for Studies on New Religions*, 1, last modified March 17, 1999, https://www.cesnur.org/testi/goXgold_01.htm. Melinda Fish, writer for *Spread the Fire* in 1999, corroborates this statement as quoted by Richard J. Smith in his article, "A Consideration of the Toronto Blessing," Didaskalia (Otterburne, Manitoba) 112, no. 1 (Fall 1999), 28.

[12] Andrew Strom, *Kundalini Warning: Are False Spirits Invading the Church?* E-book. (RevivalSchool, 2015), 44.

[13] For instance, Hiram Pangilinan, a famous Filipino Third Wave revivalist, shared how he became involved in the ministry of revival and signs and wonders back in 2001 after being exposed to North American revivalists such as Heidi Baker, Randy Clark, and Che Ahn. Pangilinan interviewed by the author, February 27, 2018. Another Filipino minister involved in the revival movement is Apollo 'Paul' Yadao. In 2006, he shared how he got connected to Leif Hetland, who became his spiritual father, and the School of Healing of Randy Clark in Lakeville, MN. Yadao interviewed by the author, January 20, 2019.

[14] Among some of these ministers are Hiram Pangilinan, a member of Che Ahn's Harvest International Ministry of Pasadena, CA; Apollo 'Paul' Yadao, a member of Leif Hetland's Global Mission Awareness of the Apostolic Network of Global Awakening; and Miguel Que, a member of Pangilinan's Church So Blessed International and founder of Impart Supernatural School, Makati City, Philippines.

Background of the Study

The gradual increase of Filipino ministers with this revivalist spirituality is somewhat double edged. On the one hand, churches have been planted and have grown with positive impact in their communities because of their emphasis on revival and signs and wonders. On the other hand, existing Evangelical and P/C churches have been bothered by the perceived excesses coming from this revivalist spirituality.[15] I personally believe that this movement may be at the edge of a slippery slope, especially since the adhering churches' emphasis on the supernatural (even those without biblical precedence) may be precarious in the Filipino context.

Most socio-religious analysts agree that the Philippines has a 'split-level Christianity', where folk (animistic) beliefs still exist in the lower level of a double-structured religiosity.[16] A tendency towards folk Christianity endangers Filipino Christians to "slipping back into an animistic worldview" if supernatural phenomena are uncritically accepted and promoted.[17] Since, as Margaret Poloma posits, the spirituality of the TB (and revivalism churches and networks that associate with them) is a form of mysticism,[18] it may cause Filipino P/Cs to fall into esoteric forms of religiosity. Thus, for the current researcher, the uncritical proliferation and acceptance of this type of spirituality is precarious for the Filipino P/C movement.

---

[15] For instance, the US Assemblies of God released a position paper warning against revival extremes and manifestation-centered ministries of contemporary revivalism. See General Presbytery of the Assemblies of God, "Endtime Revival--Spirit-Led and Spirit-Controlled: A Response Paper to Resolution 16," 2000, 1-8, https://ag.org/Beliefs/Topics-Index/Revival-Endtime-Revival--Spirit-Led-and-Spirit-Controlled (accessed January 10, 2019).

[16] Jong Fil Kim's Ph.D. dissertation surmises that Christianity in the Philippines has two levels. The upper level is composed of traditional and/or orthodox Christians (Roman Catholics and Protestants), while the lower level is composed of the popular and folk (syncretistic) forms of Christianity. See Jong Fil Kim, "Contemporary Pentecostal Charismatic Movements: On a Double-Structured Religious System in Greater Metro Manila," Ph.D. Dissertation, (University of Birmingham, UK, 2004).

[17] Hwa Yung, "Pentecostalism and the Asian Church," in *Asian and Pentecostal: The Charismatic Face of Christianity in Asia*, revised edition, eds. Allan Anderson and Edmond Tang (Eugene, OR: Wipf and Stock Publishers, 2011), 45.

[18] Margaret Poloma, *Main Street Mystics: The Toronto Blessing and Reviving Pentecostalism* (Walnut Creek, CA: AltaMira Press, 2003), 22, 27-29.

Statement of the Problem

In light of the above, Filipino classical Pentecostals must have a critical understanding of TB revivalism's theology of signs and wonders—an understanding which can be gained by a qualitative study of Filipino TB revivalists and their ministries, so that propositions for an appropriate response can be developed.

Research Questions

For this purpose, the research aimed to answer the following main question: What is a TB revivalist theology of signs and wonders from a Filipino perspective? To help answer that question, the study also aimed to address these two sub-questions: What contributed to the development of this theology in the Philippines? And, what are the implications of this theology in the Filipino P/C context?

Hypothesis of the Study

As a working hypothesis, this study posits that TB revivalism's signs and wonders theology in the Filipino perspective is similar to the signs and wonders theology espoused by the mid-1990's North American TB revivalism. The following three reasons support this hypothesis: (1) Filipino revivalists have been influenced by and are connected to North American TB revivalists; (2) both Filipino revivalists and North American TB revivalists' theologies are composed of the same interrelating themes; and, (3) both accept sub-biblical phenomena as normative manifestations of signs and wonders.

Purpose of the Study

Apart from the goal of gathering relevant information for the Filipino P/C movement, this research was conducted so that TB revivalism's signs and wonders theology is presented and explained from a Filipino perspective. The research also aimed to help Filipino classical Pentecostals have an informed understanding of the historical and theological developments that contributed to TB revivalism in the country. Lastly, I believe that the proper unveiling of TB revivalism's signs and wonders theology will be beneficial for avoiding unnecessary misunderstanding in the Filipino P/C movement.

Contribution of the Study

This research contributes to the unfinished theological task of the Pentecostal/Charismatic Movement in the Philippines. To date, there have been no academic studies conducted for the purpose of critically understanding the signs and wonders theology of TB revivalists in the country. The meaningful studies on the Philippines' P/C movement have so far focused on issues of contextualization, socio-anthropology, spirituality, social action, history, and the like.[19] Moreover, Wonsuk Ma's contribution to the *International Dictionary of Pentecostal and Charismatic Movements for the Philippines* does not include a discussion of ministries espousing this revivalist spirituality.[20] Such may be due to the lack of resources on this growing movement in the Philippines at the time of his writing.

Thus, there is a need to fill this lacuna with a research that specifically describes TB revivalism in the Philippines, as well as one that discusses its signs and wonders theology from a Filipino perspective. This is the contribution of the research.

Definition of Terms Used in the Study

Pentecostal (Neo- and Classical)

This term is defined here as "a Christian who believes that the book of Acts provides a model for the contemporary church and, on this basis, encourages every believer to experience a baptism in the Spirit (Acts 2:4), understood as an empowering for mission, distinct from regeneration that is marked by speaking in tongues, and affirms that signs and wonders, including all of the gifts listed in 1 Corinthians 12:8-

---

[19] A review of related literature on this subject will reveal the lacuna; this will be presented in Chapter 2.
[20] Wonsuk Ma, *TNIDPCM*, 204.

10, are to characterize the life of the church today."²¹ However, due to the emergence of new movements under the Pentecostal wave, this definition needs to be distinguished from the more current stream called 'neo-Pentecostal'. These are ones who agree and act according to the definition above, except that they do not affirm speaking in tongues as a normative sign for Spirit baptism.²² To distinguish between the two, the term 'classical Pentecostal' will be used in this study to refer to those who adhere to the entire tenets above, including the affirmation of speaking in tongues as the normative sign of Spirit baptism.²³

Charismatic

This term refers to "a Christian who believes that all of the gifts listed in 1 Corinthians 12:8-10, including prophecy, tongues, and healing, are available for the Church today but rejects the affirmation that baptism in the Spirit (Acts 2:4) is an empowering for mission distinct from regeneration."²⁴ These gifts are present across mainline non-Pentecostal denominations, like the Roman Catholic, Episcopalian, and other mainline Protestant churches, and even Orthodox churches.²⁵

Neo-Charismatic and Third Wave

This term refers to various independent, indigenous, and/or post-denominational Christians who believe in the continued supernatural work of the Holy Spirit in their life and community but are not clearly identified as either Pentecostal or Charismatic.²⁶ They believe in multiple infillings of the Holy Spirit, although most do not recognize a Spirit-baptism subsequent to conversion, or speaking in tongues as initial

---

[21] Robert P. Menzies, *Pentecost: This Story Is Our Story* (Springfield, MO: Gospel Publishing House, 2013), 13.
[22] Ibid., 13.
[23] *TNIDPCM* also identifies Classical Pentecostals as those affirming the essential doctrine of tongues as normative evidence of Spirit Baptism. See Vinson Synan, "Classical Pentecostalism," in *TNIDPCM*, 553.
[24] Menzies, *Pentecost*, 13.
[25] For a fuller discussion, see P.D. Hocken, "Charismatic Movement," in *TNIDPCM*, 477-519.
[26] Vinson Synan, "The Charismatic Renewal After Fifty Years," in *Spirit-Empowered Christianity in the Twenty-First Century: Insights, Analysis, and Future Trends from World-Renowned Scholars* (Lake Mary, FL: Charisma House, 2011), 16-15; cf. Stanley Burgess, "Neocharismatics," in *TNIDPCM*, 928.

evidence of Spirit-baptism.[27] Under this group is John Wimber's Association of Vineyard Churches, which Peter Wagner also called the 'Third Wave of the Holy Spirit'.[28] Vinson Synan notes that, "The ranks of the neo-Charismatic movements expanded greatly during the1990s with the advent of the Toronto Blessing movement in 1993 [sic] and the Brownsville revival in Florida in 1995."[29]

Pentecostal/Charismatic (P/C)

This term is used as a catch-all description for believers belonging to any of the three waves of the Holy Spirit Renewal.[30] Although tensions and differences abound among them, Barrett says, "All three waves share the common belief and experience of the infilling power of the Holy Spirit."[31] He further explains that the three waves are different yet closely related because they come from the same tide of Holy Spirit renewal.[32]

Evangelical

This is defined as believers coming from different traditions (e.g., Holiness, Reformed, Anabaptist, P/C) united amid their diversity as to the following evangelical distinctives:
(1) *Conversionism*—the belief that lives need to be transformed through a 'born-again' experience and a life-long process of following Jesus; (2) *Activism*—the expression and demonstration of the Gospel in missionary and social reform efforts; (3) *Biblicism*—a high regard for and obedience

---

[27]Synan, "The Charismatic Renewal After Fifty Years," 17. Cf. Todd Johnson, "The Demographics of Renewal," in *Spirit-Empowered Christianity in the Twenty-First Century* (Lake Mary, FL: Charisma House, 2011), 60.

[28]Wonsuk Ma, "A 'First Waver' Looks at the 'Third Wave': A Pentecostal Reflection on Charles Kraft's Power Encounter Terminology," *Pneuma* 19, no. 2 (Fall 1997): 189.

[29]Synan, "The Charismatic Renewal After Fifty Years," 17.

[30]The term Pentecostal/Charismatic was widely used by scholars in the 1990s to describe the global Spirit-renewal movement. This was because Pentecostals in those days began using the term Charismatic to describe their ministries, resulting in both words becoming informally synonymous in meaning. See Ibid., 15–16.

[31]David B. Barrett, "The Worldwide Holy Spirit Renewal," in *A Century of the Holy Spirit: 100 Years of Pentecostal and Charismatic Renewal*, ed.Vinson Synan (Nashville, TN: Thomas Nelson, 2001), 381.

[32]Ibid., 382.

to the Bible as the ultimate authority; and (4) *Crucicentrism*—a stress on the sacrifice of Jesus Christ on the cross as making possible the redemption of humanity.[33] These four distinctives are shared by a broad-spectrum of churches and ministries worldwide.

Toronto Blessing Revivalism

This term is used to refer to a narrow stream of P/C ministers or revivalists who utilize efforts in cultivating and preparing for a revival. TB stands for the Toronto Blessing, which means that this type of revivalism is connected to what CTF Toronto experienced back in 1994. TB revivalists are different from Protestant evangelical revivalists like Charles Finney and Dwight L. Moody, whose primary interest was in producing converts en masse.[34] TB revivalism's primary interest is a cathartic experience of God's manifest presence, which may result in epi-phenomena, such as healing/deliverance, somatic displays, and glory manifestations (e.g. gold dust, gold teeth filling, seeing angel feathers, angel orbs, etc.).

Signs and Wonders

This is defined here as "miraculous manifestations of the Holy Spirit so apparent in the 1st-century Church."[35] In the New Testament, they often refer to miracles that accompany God's salvific activity in those who accept the Gospel with faith.[36]

Other Key Terms

Theology – The study of God and his revelation to man.

---

[33]National Association of Evangelicals, "What Is an Evangelical," NAE.net, https://www.nae.net/what-is-an-evangelical (accessed December 6, 2018); cf. David W. Bebbington, *Evangelicalism in Modern Britain: A History from the 1730s to the 1930s* (London, UK: Unwin Hyman, 1989).

[34]David W. Bebbington, "What is Revivalism?" in *Christianity Today* issue 25, 1990, https://www.christianitytoday.com/history/issues/issue-25/what-is-revivalism.html (accessed January 26, 2019).

[35]Stanley Burgess and Gary McGee, "Signs and Wonders," *TNIDPCM* (Grand Rapids, MI: Zondervan, 2003), 1063.

[36]Benny Aker, "The Gospel in Action," in *Signs and Wonders in Ministry Today*, eds. Benny Aker and Gary McGee (Springfield, MO: Gospel Publishing House, 1996), 42.

Spirituality – "A quest for a fulfilled and authentic Christian existence that in the Charismatic narrative includes a process of search for God, encountered through the Holy Spirit that leads to transformation in the person and communities concerned."[37]

Filipino – A native or national of the Philippines with Filipino ancestry, speaking its national language, and adhering to Filipino cultural values (e.g., family/community orientation, patron system).

Filipino classical Pentecostal – A Filipino Christian who adheres to the basic doctrines of evangelicalism with the added classical Pentecostal distinctives listed above. In this study, the Filipino classical Pentecostals will be represented by the Assemblies of God (AG) in the Philippines, which, although greatly influenced by North American Assemblies of God missionaries, was still essentially formed by Filipino-American *balikbayans* (returnees).[38] Aside from distinctive Filipino values, they differ from the West because inherent in their worldview is the acceptance of a supernatural world that can affect their this-worldly affairs.[39]

Unusual – Aberrant or straying from the norm. In this study, since the Bible is the *norma normans* (the standard norm for faith and practice), the phenomenon, which may be claimed as a manifestation of signs and wonders yet not mentioned in the Bible, is considered an unusual manifestation of signs and wonders.

Normative – A theological term that refers to confessions or claims that are considered true always and for everyone because they are derived from Scripture (the primary rule of faith).

Non-normative – A theological term that refers to confessions or claims that are not considered true always and for everyone because of their subjectivity and insufficient biblical support.

Indigenous – A word that means native.

---

[37] Mark Cartledge, *Encountering the Spirit: The Charismatic Tradition* (London, Darton, UK: Longman and Todd, 2006), 26.

[38] Conrado Lumahan, "Facts and Figures: A History of the Growth of the Philippine Assemblies of God," *Asian Journal of Pentecostal Studies* 8, no. 2 (2005), 340-344.

[39] Rodney L. Henry, *Filipino Spirit World: A Challenge to the Church* (Manila, Philippines: OMF Literature, 1986), 8, 13; cf. Dave Johnson, *Theology in Context: A Case Study in the Philippines* (Baguio, Philippines: APTS Press, 2013), 45.

Assumptions Made in the Study

In carrying out this study, the researcher made the following nine assumptions:

- The Bible is the supreme authority for faith and practice and it is the primary source of theology.
- Signs and wonders can either witness to the Good News of God's Kingdom (Matthew 12:28) or can be a deception of the enemy (2 Thessalonians 2:9).
- Since the researcher is a Filipino from the classical Pentecostal stream (Assemblies of God), signs and wonders are part of the works of the Holy Spirit for the proclamation of the Gospel in these last days.
- Believers involved in P/C revivalism are Spirit-empowered Christians.
- This study will be helpful for the P/C movement in the Philippines, since it contributes relevant information to the growing Spirit-empowered movements in the country.
- Although God can move in many ways miraculously, he has revealed in the Bible and through the history of the Church that there are salvific and edifying purposes to his flexibility and creativity in the supernatural.
- The word "critical" does not refer to destructive criticism, but rather means being reflective, analytical, and constructive. (The goal here is to increase understanding, air out agreements and disagreements, and foster rapprochement.)
- Those involved in TB revivalism believe in the manifestation of signs and wonders as earthly manifestations of the glory of God.
- There is a relationship between the Filipino supernatural worldview and the Filipinos' openness to the moving of the Holy Spirit in signs and wonders.

Scope and Limitations of the Study

Due to time and space constraints, this paper focused on understanding TB revivalism's signs and wonders theology from the Filipino context. Special focus was given to supernatural manifestations that do not have biblical precedent (otherwise identified as 'unusual signs and wonders' or 'glory manifestations').

First, data gathering was limited to only four TB revivalists and their respective ministries in the Philippines. These four were chosen based on their influence in promoting TB revivalism in the country. Interviews were conducted to understand their personal and ministerial history, as well as their theology of signs and wonders.

Second, because I belong to the Assemblies of God in the Philippines, critiques and analysis came from a classical Pentecostal perspective.

Third, the literature and studies review in Chapter 2 discussed literature and studies covering the development of TB revivalism mostly coming from North America until it reached the Philippines. The review also included a brief cultural and religious exegesis of Filipino Christianity.

Fourth, the study was limited to a discussion of TB revivalists' understanding of the manifestation of unusual signs and wonders (or glory manifestations), such as gold dust, angel feathers, heavenly gemstones, etc. Other controversial issues raised by TB revivalism's theologies (e.g., deliverance, somatic displays, making animal sounds, spiritual warfare, inner healing, demonology) are too broad and thus beyond the scope of this research.

Chapter 2

Review of Literature on the Toronto Blessing Revivalism

Renewalism, Revivalism and the Toronto Blessing

The Three Waves of Holy Spirit Renewal

Spirit-Empowered Christianity (or the Pentecostal/Charismatic Movement) has spread throughout the world, having the potential to reshape the Christian religion in the 21st century.[1] It reached the Philippines beginning in the 1920s, when North American missionaries, as well as Filipino *balikbayans*[2] who experienced the modern Pentecostal revival, brought its message to the country.[3] One of its hallmarks is 'renewalist spirituality'[4]—i.e., a belief in the continued work of the Holy Spirit in individuals and communities through an encounter with God and His spiritual gifts. This spirituality has also contributed to a renewal ecclesiology. John Lyons explains that with this ecclesiology, "Believers see the church as continually in need of renewal, a process which eventually can be seen as a series of revival events or 'waves.'"[5] This

---

[1] Harvey Cox, *Fire From Heaven: The Rise of Pentecostal Spirituality and the Reshaping of Christianity in the Twenty-First Century* (New York, NY: Addison-Wesley, 2001); David Martin, *Pentecostalism: The World Their Parish* (Oxford, UK: Blackwell Publishers, 2002).

[2] A *balikbayan* is a Filipino visiting or returning to the Philippines after a period of living in another country. See *Oxford Dictionaries, s.v.,* "balikbayan," https://en.oxforddictionaries.com/definition/balikbayan (accessed February 7, 2019).

[3] Wonsuk Ma, "Philippines," in *The New International Dictionary of Pentecostal and Charismatic Movements*, revised and expanded. (Grand Rapids, MI: Zondervan, 2003), 201.

[4] Todd Johnson, "The Demographics of Renewal," 60.

[5] John Lyons, "The Fourth Wave and the Approaching Millennium: Some Problems with Charismatic Hermeneutics," *ANVIL* 15, no. 3 (1998), 170.

view is best exemplified by the P/C Movement's historical purview of the 'three waves of Holy Spirit renewal' from the 1900s.[6]

Vinson Synan explains that in North America, P/C renewalism began with the first wave of the modern Pentecostal revival in the early 1900 to the second wave of the Charismatic Renewal in the 1960s and to the third wave of the neo-Charismatics in the 1980s.[7] Following this North American purview, P/C scholars likewise explain establishment of the Pentecostal movement in the Philippines in three waves.[8] The first wave began in the late 1920s (augmented by a national revival in the 1950s, called the Manila Pentecostal Revival);[9] the second wave was the Charismatic Renewal in the 1970s;[10] and the third wave was when the Neo-Charismatics entered the scene in the late 1980s to the early 1990s.[11] The existence of these three waves provides a rich diversity, resulting in the formation of distinct and continuing streams within the Church in the Philippines and beyond.

---

[6]Vinson Synan, *The Century of the Holy Spirit: 100 Years of Pentecostal and Charismatic Renewal 1901-2001* (Nashville, TN: Thomas Nelson, 2001), 9–10.

[7]Synan, "The Charismatic Renewal After Fifty Years," 17.

[8]Jae Yong Jeong affirms that Pentecostalism developed in a similar fashion to the North American P/C Movement because of the influence of missionaries. See Jae Yong Jeong, "Filipino Pentecostal Spirituality: An Investigation into Filipino Indigenous Spirituality and Pentecostalism in the Philippines" (Ph.D. Dissertation, University of Birmingham, UK, 2001), 10.

[9]Wonsuk Ma, "Philippines," 201; (Elijah) Jong Fil Kim, "Contemporary Pentecostal Charismatic Movements on a Double Structured Religious System in Greater Manila Area" (Ph.D. Dissertation, University of Birmingham, UK, 2004), 227-228.

[10]Wonsuk Ma, "Philippines," 204-207.

[11]Kim identifies the neo-Charismatics or Third Wavers as indigenous, autochthonous, and independent churches observing P/C-like traditions without being clearly identified as Pentecostal or Charismatic. He posits that they began in the 1980s and 90s. See Kim, "Contemporary Pentecostal Charismatic Movements on a Double Structured Religious System in Greater Manila Area," 80. It must be noted, however, that post-denominationalists experiencing the main phenomenological hallmarks of Pentecostalism should be included in this list. See Johnson, "The Demographics of Renewal," 60.

With this renewalist spirituality in the P/C Movement, it is not surprising that, in the mid-1990s, a new stream emerged from the West as a result of a search for fresh experiences of spiritual power.[12]

New Stream of Renewal: the Toronto Blessing

In 1994, Catch the Fire (CTF) church in Toronto became the center of a pilgrimage by almost two million people who wanted to experience a modern-day revival. British media dubbed the phenomena associated with CTF as the "Toronto Blessing."[13] Percy explained that the TB became famous because of a high reportage of emotional outbursts, ecstatic somatic displays, and unusual phenomena, which were anecdotally expressed as "more highly-charged than anything that had preceded it."[14] John D. Hannah called it a "manifestation of charismatic renewalism,"[15] while those involved in the TB described it as a revival, in continuity with the 18th century awakenings.[16]

Mark Stibbe, in attempting a prophetic exegesis of Ezekiel 47, proposed that the TB was the beginning of a fourth wave of the Holy Spirit renewal, which would lead to a worldwide church revival.[17] This was contradicted by some scholars like Lyons, who critiqued Stibbe's overall claims based on problematic exegesis and insufficient grounds

---

[12]Hilborn, using various sources, chronicled the pre-history the TB. He was able to chronicle the search for a new anointing or spiritual power of two TB leaders—Randy Clark and John Arnott. In August 1993, Clark participated in a Rodney Howard-Browne meeting, where he received "tremendous power." Arnott, wanting to experience the Argentinian revival, flew to Argentina for the Harvest Evangelism Pastor's Conference in October/November 1994. There he was prayed over by Claudio Friedzon. Both Clark and Arnott were actively searching for higher levels of anointing for their ministries. See David Hilborn, ed., *"Toronto" in Perspective: Papers on the New Charismatic Wave of the Mid 1990s* (Carlisle, UK: Paternoster Press, 2001), 145–146.

[13]Ruth Gledhill of the *London Times* was the first to publicly label the religious phenomena at CTF in her article published on June 18, 1994. See Ibid., 4.

[14]Martyn Percy, "Adventure and Atrophy in a Charismatic Movement: Returning to the 'Toronto Blessing,'"*Journal of Contemporary Religion* 20, no. 1 (2005): 71-72; Hunt, "The 'Toronto Blessing,'" 258.

[15]John Hannah, "Jonathan Edwards, The Toronto Blessing, and The Spiritual Gifts: Are the Extraordinary Ones Actually the Ordinary Ones?" *Trinity Journal* 17, no. 2 (1996), 167.

[16]Guy Chevreau, *Catch the Fire*, Reprint. (Toronto, Ontario: HarperCollins Publishers, 1995), 212-222.

[17]Mark Stibbe, *Times of Refreshing: A Practical Theology of Revival* (London, UK: Marshall Pickering, 1995), 170-180.

for discernment.[18] In the end, the TB and the churches and networks that followed it were never globally known as a fourth wave of the Holy Spirit in the P/C tradition. Instead, Cartledge posited that they were best described as a revivalist spirituality, motivated by their own "spirituality process of search-encounter-transformation."[19]

Evangelical Revivalism Versus TB Revivalism

Their revivalist spirituality though is best identified within a tradition of Protestant Evangelicalism known as revivalism.[20] In simple terms, revivalism is a type of activism wherein one employs efforts to produce converts and reawaken the Christian life.[21] Charles Finney became the most famous proponent of this tradition in the 18th century when he employed "new measures"—i.e., systems or techniques of stimulating and emotionally directing people to respond to the gospel.[22] Finney was not alone in observing this tradition. Years later Dwight L. Moody, Billy Graham, and even the German Pentecostal Reinhard Bonnke and others became famous Evangelical revivalists.

However, the stream of revivalism coming from the TB is different from Protestant Evangelical Revivalism.[23] While the goals of the former are the "revitalization and expansion of the church,"[24] TB Revivalism espouses a more romantic and mystical purpose. CTF founder John Arnott described the heart of his church's tradition as "a call to romance, a call to having an intimate relationship with Jesus."[25] This 'divine romance' is usually manifested in somatic displays, epi-phenomena, and

---

[18]Lyons, "The Fourth Wave and the Approaching Millennium: Some Problems with Charismatic Hermeneutics," 175-180.

[19]Cartledge, "'Catch the Fire': Revivalist Spirituality from Toronto to Beyond," 237.

[20]David Hilborn, Introduction: Evangelicalism, the Evangelical Alliance and the Toronto Blessing," in "Toronto" in Perspective: Papers on the New Charismatic Wave of the Mid 1990s, ed. David Hilborn (Carlisle, UK: Paternoster Press, 2001), 12-14.

[21]David Bebbington, "What Is Revivalism?" *Christianity Today*, 1990, https://www.christianitytoday.com/history/issues/issue-25/what-is-revivalism.html (accessed February 6, 2019).

[22]Iain Murray, *Revival and Revivalism: The Making and Marring of Evangelical Revivalism 1750-1858* (Carlisle, PA: Banner of Truth, 1994), xviii, 237–250.

[23]William G. McLoughlin, *Modern Revivalism: Charles Grandison Finney to Billy Graham* (New York, NY: Ronald Press, 1959).

[24]Hilborn, "Introduction," 13.

[25]John Arnott, *The Father's Blessing* (Orlando, FL: Creation House, 1995), 17.

experiences of what Dixon called "altered states of Christian consciousnesses."[26] Martyn Percy, in a follow-up visit to CTF (Toronto Airport Christian Fellowship at the time of his writing), remarked about their meetings that "The operant stress is on tactile, almost romantic somatic encounters with God, which lead to deep cathartic spiritual moments, which in turn provide liberating and generative possibilities for individual spiritual renewal and further empowerment."[27]

Although the romantic overtones and ecstatic phenomena described in their assemblies are not new for those in the P/C Movement,[28] what marked it for special consideration was the observation that these have become a primal core in their spirituality. Kydd posits that participants of events like TB-meetings "have focused, perhaps fixated, on highly charged moments of great spiritual intensity."[29] Their meetings have greater emphasis on spiritual/emotional healing, deliverance, and exotic spiritual epi-phenomena (e.g., gold teeth filling, gold dusting). Percy also noticed that, years after the TB, "the romantic element had become even more explicit and intense."[30]

In studying the TB at Arnott's church, Poloma suggested that the heart of their process is spiritual healing.[31] People who come to the TB or a TB-like meeting testify to cathartic experiences (e.g., receiving divine forgiveness, restoration, emotional healing, deeper sensitivity to the Lord, being more in love with God, and being delivered from sinful bondage).[32] It can be further inferred from Arnott's teaching that the experience of such manifestations as smelling supernatural fragrance in an assembly,[33] seeing angels (or hearing rumors of angels),[34] seeing a cloud fill a worship-space,[35] and witnessing gold tooth-filling and gold

---

[26]Patrick Dixon, *Signs of Revival* (Eastbourne, UK: Kingsway Publications, 1994), 258-260.
[27]Percy, "Adventure and Atrophy," 78.
[28]Kydd comments that the manifestations associated with the TB are not without precedent but are more like reruns. See Ronald Kydd, "A Retrospectus/Prospectus on Physical Phenomena Centered on the 'Toronto Blessing,'" *Journal of Pentecostal Theology* 6, no. 12 (1998), 77.
[29]Kydd., 80.
[30]Percy, "Adventure and Atrophy," 79.
[31]Margaret Poloma, "Inspecting the Fruit of the 'Toronto Blessing': A Sociological Perspective," *Pneuma: The Journal of the Society for Pentecostal Studies* 20, no. 1 (Spring 1998), 69.
[32]Ibid., 57–64.
[33]Arnott, *The Father's Blessing*, 155-156.
[34]Hunt, "The 'Toronto Blessing,'" 258.
[35]Hilborn, *"Toronto,"* 227.

dusting,³⁶ serve to deepen intimacy with God and people.³⁷ However, only a small percent of participants in their meetings (1% in Poloma's sample) made first-time commitments to Jesus.³⁸

These observations led many Evangelicals to identify the TB not as a revival experience (because it did not lead to mass conversion), but rather as a renewal or a revivalism—i.e., a preparation for revival.³⁹ For many, the TB fell short of a true revival since it had minimal conversions and had no effect on society at large. This supposition prompted scholars like Tim Thornborough, Gethin Russell-Jones, and Andrew Walker to point out that the TB came closer to revivalism than true revival.⁴⁰ Rob Warner's comment further explains:

> Toronto came in with a bang but frankly, seems to have ended with a whimper. For me, it was a time of deep spiritual enrichment and rekindled hope for revival. Yet it was also a time of being turned off by the threefold ministries of unreality—exaggeration, manipulation and hysteria... Perhaps Toronto is best seen as a parable of the mixed brew that is renewal.⁴¹

John Wimber, the founder of Vineyard, agrees with this description, having identified the TB phenomenon and others like it simply as a renewal.⁴² However, Arnott and those in his network disagree and insist that they have been and still are 'hosting a revival'.⁴³

---

³⁶Percy, "Adventure and Atrophy," 72.
³⁷Arnott, *The Father's Blessing*, 145-167.
³⁸Poloma, "Inspecting the Fruit of the 'Toronto Blessing'," 59.
³⁹Hilborn cites the Euston Statement of December 1994, where the Evangelical Alliance concluded that the TB is not a revival but a period of preparation for revival. See Hilborn, "Introduction," 12–13.
⁴⁰Hilborn, "Introduction," 13.
⁴¹Ibid.
⁴²John Wimber, founder and late leader of the Vineyard Association of Churches, which CTF belonged to at the time of the TB, was one of those who firmly insisted on calling the phenomena as a renewal and not a revival. See Bill Jackson, *The Quest for the Radical Middle: A History of the Vineyard*, Kindle. (Capetown, South Africa: Vineyard International Publishing, 2010), 3990.
⁴³Arnott calls the CTF revival as "The Father's Heart Revival (Toronto)." See John and Carol Arnott, *Preparing for the Glory: Getting Ready for the Next Wave of Holy Spirit Outpouring*. (Shippensburg, PA: Destiny Image Publishers, Inc., 2018), 121, Kindle.

Revival: Differing Definitions

The debate as to whether the TB and those like it are considered a revival or not may come from different definitions of the term 'revival'. Bethel (Redding, CA), an internationally known TB revivalist church, defines revival in its webpage as "the personal, regional, and global expansion of God's kingdom through His manifest presence."[44] The 'manifest presence' referred to here is the "reality of heaven on earth"— i.e., miracles and supernatural living put on display.[45] This revival, says Bill Johnson (senior leader at Bethel) should be a normal daily expectation of believers and be as natural as breathing.[46]

Johnson's description of revival, however, is different from the Protestant Evangelical description, that being "a 'surprising and special season of God.'"[47] Revivals have been viewed traditionally as spontaneous events, a sovereign work of God with a redemptive purpose.[48] Moreover, for Evangelicals, the principle of ebb and flow operates in revival history.[49] Tom Phillips writes:

> Like a wave, revival will crest at some point. The culmination will be relatively short before the wave follows its natural course and recedes. It's impossible to live "at the peak" or "on the crest" forever. A revival will move us to new heights and revitalize us. Like reaching the top of a mountain, we know our time on the summit is limited. The time comes to move on. The exhilaration of the view is what inspires us when we go back down to live in the valley. This is the ebb and flow of revival; spiritual awakening itself lasts only briefly but its impact can linger much longer.[50]

---

[44]"Our Mission," Bethel, https://www.bethel.com/about (accessed February 11, 2019).

[45]Bill Johnson, *The Supernatural Power of a Transformed Mind: Access to a Life of Miracles* (Shippensburg, PA: Destiny Image Publishers, Inc., 2005), 34-35.

[46]Bill Johnson, *The Supernatural Power*, 156.

[47]Murray, *Revival and Revivalism*, xvii, 19-21.

[48]Tom Phillips, *Revival Signs: Join the New Spiritual Awakening* (Gresham, OR: Vision House Publishing, Inc., 1995), 211-212.

[49]Ibid., 208-209, 212-213.

[50]Ibid., 210.

Hence, the idea of living in a continual state of revival, the manifestations of which are displays of signs and wonders and supernatural living, is incongruent with the traditional view of revival and is somewhat paradoxical to daily living.

Typologies of Revivalism

Due to the awkwardness of identifying a revival, Latham proposes a typology indicating six senses of revival, which is based on the idea that revivalism is an intentional cultivation of a special move of God (see Table 1).[51]

Table 1. Latham's Revivalism Typology.

R1	A spiritual quickening of the individual believer.
R2	A deliberate meeting or campaign especially among Pentecostals
R3	An unplanned period of spiritual enlivening in a local church, quickening believers and bringing unbelievers to faith.
R4	A regional experience of spiritual awakening and widespread conversion (e.g., the Welsh, Hebridean, East African, and Indonesian revivals—and possibly Pensacola in the 1990s).
R5	Societal or cultural "awakenings" (e.g., the transatlantic First and Second Awakenings)
R6	The possible reversal of secularization and "revival" of Christianity as such.

---

[51] Steve Latham, "'God Came from Teman': Revival and Contemporary Revivalism," in *On Revival: A Critical Examination*, ed. Andrew Walker and Kristine Aune (Carlisle, UK: Paternoster Press, 2003), 172; cf. Cartledge, "'Catch the Fire': Revivalist Spirituality from Toronto to Beyond," 226.

Although Latham's revivalism typology helps in seeing the semantic range of the term 'revival', Cartledge considers it insufficient in describing revivalism in the P/C tradition.[52] He notes that Latham's typology fits a more non-Pentecostal Evangelical view, does not consider the P/C feature of spiritual empowerment (e.g., ecstatic phenomena, spiritual gifts, miracles), does not "reference networks of revival," and has a more "geographically contained understanding of its boundaries."[53] Thus he proposes a revision of Latham's typology that fits P/C spirituality, particularly that of CTF and its network (see Table 2).[54]

Table 2. Cartledge's Revivalism Typology.

R1	A spiritual enlivening and empowering of the individual believer.
R2	A deliberate meeting or campaign to deepen the faith of believers and bring non-believers to faith and experience the power of God in their lives.
R3	A period of spiritual intensity that enlivens a congregation such that the body of believers is empowered and witnesses claim to experience mass conversions, healings and miracles (Catch the Fire 1994).
R4	News on the enlivening spreads so that the congregation becomes a site of spiritual pilgrimage, nationally, and internationally (CTF 1995 and 1996).
R5	The congregation expands, becomes an international denomination or network of both (CTF 1996).
R6	The network collaborates internationally with other similar networks to spread revivalist spirituality globally (CTF and Revival Alliance from 2011).
R7	The network impacts the political and cultural influence of Christianity locally, nationally, regionally, and globally.

---

[52] Cartledge, "'Catch the Fire': Revivalist Spirituality from Toronto to Beyond," 226.
[53] Ibid.
[54] Ibid., 225-226, 232.

According to this typology, CTF and other churches and networks that practice revivalism have reached an R6-sense of revival but have yet to reach R7.[55] It is probably their failure to reach R7 (i.e., a sense of revival comparable to a Great Awakening or a revival of Christianity), which has caused many to view them as falling short of a historic revival. Martin Davie, who considers the Toronto experience as "an extremely significant turning point" in history, likewise concluded that the TB had not produced the "wave of revival hoped for by many in 1994 and 1995."[56] Poloma also commented that the TB in North America "seems to be stuck in an independent stream in the P/C Movement . . . having little impact on the larger Church or among the growing numbers of unchurched in American society."[57]

Thus, for these independent stream of TB revivalists, there is a challenge to make a centrifugal (societal and global) Christian impact so that they can reify their claims of 'hosting a revival.'

Summary

The review above delves into a revivalist spirituality that began in the mid-1990s. Although in previous years this spirituality was observed in the fringes of P/C meetings all over the world, it was during the 'Toronto Blessing' that these phenomena came prominent in a Charismatic renewal meeting. Evangelicals, even those within P/C circles, considered it controversial because of the intensity and bizarreness of manifestations that were previously relegated to the fringes. It continued to make waves in Evangelical discussion because of its proponents' insistence that the phenomenon was a revival, not just a renewal. In fact, Arnott labeled it 'the Father's Heart Revival', in connection to 18th century revivals and the modern Pentecostal revival.[58] Most Evangelicals, however, viewed it more as revivalism—a preparation for revival.

---

[55]Cartledge, "'Catch the Fire': Revivalist Spirituality from Toronto to Beyond," 232.

[56]Martin Davie, "A Real but Limited Renewal," in *"Toronto" in Perspective,* 42.

[57]Poloma, "Inspecting the Fruit of the 'Toronto Blessing'," 69.

[58]Arnott, *Preparing for the Glory,* 30, 121.

Chapter 3

Review of Literature on Historical Roots and Theological Antecedents

Historical Roots of Toronto Blessing Revivalism

This type of revivalism did not come from a vacuum. Davie considers it a "development of the 'Pentecostal-charismatic' tradition within worldwide Christianity,"[1] while Poloma identifies it as "the latest phase of the pentecostal/charismatic (p/c) movement."[2] Pawson traces its roots back to the 1901 Topeka, Kansas, revival.[3]

David Hilborn in his book, *'Toronto' in Perspective*, successfully presented a historical chronology of the development of this revivalism.[4] Hilborn, who identified the TB and the resulting revivalist movement as a "crisis for modern-day evangelicalism,"[5] produced a most exhaustive background on the genesis and development of the TB by compiling articles, books, reports, statements, and other literature on the topic from 1954 (its pre-history) to 2000 (year of decline/transmutation). To date, there is no other academic treatise that traces the TB's development and transmutation into a revivalist movement as exhaustive as Hilborn's work.

Due to space constraints, this chapter will not discuss the literature and studies that trace the movement's historical roots. Instead, using Hilborn's chronology plus other supporting sources, a concise historical

---

[1]Davie, "A Real but Limited Renewal," 36.
[2]Margaret Poloma, "The 'Toronto Blessing': Charisma, Institutionalization, and Revival," *Journal for the Scientific Study of Religion* 36, no. 2 (June 1997), 257.
[3]Pawson, "A Mixed Blessing," in *"Toronto" in Perspective*, 83.
[4]Hilborn, ed., "Part II: A Chronicle of the Toronto Blessing," in *"Toronto" in Perspective*, 131-330.
[5]Hilborn, "Introduction," 3.

outline of the TB's development into a global revivalist movement will be presented (see Table 3).[6]

Table 3. Historical Chronology of Western TB Revivalism.

YEAR	TABLE OF WESTERN TB HISTORY
Pre-History of TB Revivalism	
1901	The Topeka, Kansas, Revival (Charles Parham) results in formulation of the doctrine of tongues as initial evidence (i.e., Spirit baptism a post-conversion experience initially evidenced by speaking in tongues). Parham was able to connect the baptism experience with a theology. Although his Apostolic Faith movement did not gain worldwide recognition, one of his students, Seymour, became a catalyst for spread of the modern Pentecostal revival.[7]
1906	The Azusa Street Revival (William Seymour) brings the Pentecostal revival worldwide recognition as leaders around the world experience it and receive Spirit baptism at Seymour's Azusa Street Apostolic Faith Mission. It was noted for interracial harmony and for having an emphasis on repentance, holiness, and the lordship of Jesus.[8]
1930	Kathryn Kuhlman gains recognition by opening the Denver Revival Tabernacle. She was a Neo-Pentecostal, who later influenced Benny Hinn.
January 1948	Healing Revivals under William Branham and Oral Roberts gain a following. These revivals would later become influential to the Latter Rain Movement and most notably the Charismatic Renewal.
February 1948	The Latter Rain Movement begins.[9] "Leaders in the movement interpret Acts 2 and the 'latter rain' to

---

[6]The items listed in the table are from Hilborn's chronology. Some are taken from other sources and referenced accordingly. Unless referenced differently, the rest of the items are quoted from Hilborn's chronology. For a complete chronicle and discussion, see Hilborn, "Part II: A Chronicle of the Toronto Blessing," 131-330; cf. Vinson Synan, *In the Latter Days: The Outpouring of the Holy Spirit in the Twentieth Century*, Revised. (Ann Arbor, MI: Servant Publications, 1991); cf. Jackson, *The Quest for the Radical Middle: A History of the Vineyard*; cf. Poloma, "The 'Toronto Blessing'"; cf. R. Douglas Geivett and Holly Pivec, *A New Apostolic Reformation: A Biblical Response to a Worldwide Movement* (Wooster, OH: Weaver Book Co., 2014); and Pawson, "A Mixed Blessing," 83-85.

[7]Synan, *The Century of the Holy Spirit*, 44.

[8]Ibid., 61.

[9]George R. Hawtin, "Latter Rain Movement, 'Letter to Wayne Warner,'" in *Pentecostal and Charismatic Movements: A Reader*, ed. William K. Kay and Anne E. Dyer (London, UK: SCM Press, 1987), 19.

	refer to an end-time revival, which will begin with a dramatic surge of spiritual activity. Later, the movement would formulate a teaching called 'Manifest Sons of God,' referring to a band of new apostles whose task would be to restore the Church to a state of purity and prepare it as a spotless bride for the return of her husband, the Messiah. Key facets in the teaching include recovery of signs and wonders and imparting spiritual gifts via the laying on of hands and prophecy (i.e., through a transferable anointing)."[10]
1949	The General Council of the Assemblies of God in North America sanctioned the Latter Rain Movement and its leaders on various grounds, including elitism and an "overemphasis on imparting spiritual gifts through the laying on of hands and prophecy."[11]
January 1971	Ruth Ward Heflin claims to have been visited by the living creatures of Revelation 4:7-8 and Ezekiel 10:1. She then received a call to minister in Jerusalem.[12]
1972	Heflin moves to Jerusalem and begins a ministry of praise and intercession, with testimonies of entering into and living in the glory realm.[13]
1972	Omar Cabrera founds Visions-of-the-Future Ministry, with headquarters in Buenos Aires. He also began crusades in different locations in Argentina characterized by outward manifestations of spiritual power. Although his ministry was rejected by Evangelical leaders of the day, he was later recognized as the precursor to the Argentine Revival.[14]
1974	Benny Hinn begins to develop a self-styled 'anointed' ministry in Ontario, Canada. He forms a close friendship with John Arnott.
1981	John Wimber and the Vineyard churches gain recognition. Peter Wagner calls their movement the 'Third Wave of the Holy Spirit.'

[10] David Hilborn, ed., "The Pre-History of the Blessing," in *"Toronto" in Perspective*, 140; cf. Hawtin, "Latter Rain Movement," 20.

[11] Hilborn, "The Pre-History of the Blessing," 140.

[12] Ruth Ward Heflin, *Glory: Experiencing the Atmosphere of Heaven* (Hagerstown, MD: McDougal Publishing, 1990), ii.

[13] Ibid., 6ff.

[14] J. Gordon Melton and Clifton Holland, "Argentina," in *Religions of the World: A Comprehensive Encyclopedia of Beliefs and Practices*, ed. J. Gordon Melton and Martin Baumann, 2nd ed. (Santa Barbara, CA: ABC-CLIO, LLC, 2010), 176; C. Peter Wagner and Pablo Deiros, eds., *The Rising Revival: Firsthand Accounts of the Incredible Argentine Revival--and How It Can Spread Throughout the World* (Venture, CA: Renew Books, 1998), 19.

October 1981	Rodney Howard-Browne joins the Word of Faith Movement by studying at Rhema Church.
1982	The Great Argentine Revival begins with a citywide, inter-denominational crusade by former businessman-turned-evangelist Carlos Annacondia. He popularized the same crusade practices that Omar Cabrera pioneered. His crusades had displays of unusual phenomena and healings.[15]
1986	John and Carol Arnott attend conferences in Vancouver and Ohio led by Wimber.
1987	The Arnott's Stratford Church officially joins the Vineyard network. The Stratford was the Arnott's first church, prior to pioneering CTF (originally named Toronto Airport Vineyard).
1987	Outbreaks of 'holy laughter' manifest in Claudio Friedzon's Kings of Kings Church in Argentina.
April 1989	Rodney Howard-Browne's ministry gains significant impact, with manifestations of 'drunkenness in the Spirit' during his meetings.
1990	The Arnotts find for their burgeoning Toronto congregation rented accommodations—the end block of a warehouse/office complex near the airport. Their new name is Toronto Airport Vineyard (TAV).
1990	Ruth Ward Heflin's book, titled *Glory: Experiencing the Atmosphere of Heaven,* is first released. It contained her experiences and teachings on the glory realm and experiencing heaven's glories. According to her, the glory realm is manifestation of the reality of God's glorious presence.[16] The one who enters into and lives in it moves in mighty miracles and witness heaven's glories (e.g. seeing pillars of clouds, sparkles of gold, angels at work). She teaches that only a true worshiper enters into the glory realm.[17]

---

[15] J. Gordon Melton and Martin Baumann, eds., *Religions of the World: A Comprehensive Encyclopedia of Beliefs and Practices*, 2nd ed. (Santa Barbara, CA: ABC-CLIO, LLC, 2010), 176.
[16] Heflin, *Glory*, 133.
[17] Ibid., 79.

Spring 1992	Friedzon seeks a new anointing from Benny Hinn, returns to Kings of Kings Church, and witnesses a doubling of manifestations of laughter and 'falling under the power.'[18]
May 1992	Marc Dupont, a pastoral team member at TAV, has a detailed vision. He sees a mountain landscape in which a large amount of water is cascading onto a huge rock. He understands God to be telling him that Toronto shall be a place where much living water will flow with great power, even though at the present time both the church and the city are like big rocks, cold and hard against God's love and Spirit.
Summer 1992	Passing on oversight of the Stratford congregation to Jerry Steingrad, the Arnotts move to Toronto and focus full time on TAV. At this major crossroad in their life, the couple is keen to seek fresh empowerment from God.
Sept. 1992	The Arnotts attend a series of Benny Hinn meetings, seeking fresh anointing for their ministry at TAV.
April 1993	Rodney Howard-Browne holds revival meetings at Carpenter's Home Church in Lakeland, FL. Notable outbreaks of 'holy laughter' and 'falling' become prominent in the meeting. Browne is known as the 'Holy Spirit bartender.'
June 1993	The Arnott's attend their first Rodney Howard-Browne meeting at Fort Worth, TX.
August 1993	Close to a nervous breakdown because of a tough but relatively unfruitful ministry at the Vineyard Christian Fellowship in St. Louis, MO, Randy Clark attends a Rodney Howard-Browne meeting at Kenneth Hagin's Rhema Bible Church in Tulsa, OK. There, Clark experiences holy laughter. In subsequent meetings at Lakeland, FL, Browne ministers to Clark, who feels tremendous power come into his hands. He then returns to his church in St. Louis and reports that some 95% of his congregation 'fall under the power'.
October-Nov. 1993	The Arnott's fly to Argentina to join the Harvest Evangelism Pastor's Conference. John Arnott testifies to receiving an empowerment from Claudio Friedzon.
November 1993	Hearing about the transformation of Randy Clark's ministry and congregation. John Arnott contacts Clark and asks him to visit TAV in January.

---

[18]Richard Riss, "A History of the Awakening 1992-1995," The Revival Library, chap. 2, http://www.revival-library.org/index.php/catalogues-menu/pentecostal/a-history-of-the-awakening-of-1992-1995 (accessed February 21, 2019).

November 1993	In the United Kingdom, reports of the North American 'holy laughter' movement begin to spread as tourists and business travelers return home from trips across the Atlantic.
Rise and Spread of the 'Toronto Blessing'	
January 1994	The Toronto Blessing begins. With Randy Clark speaking at TAV's family night meeting, during prayer time the whole congregation exhibits manifestations, which were later on collectively dubbed as 'drunkenness in the Spirit.' This type of meeting became a daily service for 42 days, with Clark staying on until March 26.
February 1994	The Arnotts travel from Toronto to an out-of-town healing conference and begin to share the events in TAV. An outbreak of laughter and phenomena similar to those at TAV occurs in that conference.
March-April 1994	Randy Clark returns home to St. Louis. TAV develops a pattern of daily ministry that will soon become standard for churches operating in the same vein. Arnott forms a specially trained prayer team that works out of a *modus operandi* which includes: encouraging people to receive repeatedly from God, catching them carefully when they fall, urging them to stay on the floor and 'rest in the Spirit', interceding enthusiastically for those who are manifesting the activities associated with the new movement, and (where appropriate) explaining to those present the spiritual significance of what is going on. TAV meetings swell to over, 1,000, and a mass 'pilgrimage' from both within North America and beyond begins.
April 1994	Che Ahn has a Toronto-like experience at a conference held by John Wimber at Anaheim Vineyard that spiritually energizes him to start Vineyard in Greater Pasadena (CA). After pioneering his church, Ahn visited TAV and quickly identified with the renewal taking place.[19]
May 1994	Bill Jackson writes a paper on the TB for Champaign (IL) Vineyard church, acknowledging that the TB is a refreshing move of God, with instances of God 'manifesting His presence' (a common Vineyard parlance that refers to God's self-disclosure).[20] However, for him, the rate of conversion in TB

---

[19] Margaret Poloma, "A Reconfiguration of Pentecostalism," in *"Toronto" in Perspective,* 108.

[20] Jackson, *The Quest for the Radical Middle: A History of the Vineyard,* loc. 3828-4184. Kindle.

	meetings is not enough to characterize it as a genuine revival.[21]
May 24, 1994 11:30 a.m.	Eleanor Mumford of Southwest London Vineyard, having just returned from the TB in TAV, prays for church leaders present in a meeting at her home. While praying, Toronto-like manifestations take hold and a dramatic session occurs. Among those affected was Nicky Gumbel of Holy Trinity, Brompton (HTB), UK.
May 24, 1994 2:00 p.m.	Nicky Gumbel leaves Mumford's home to join a meeting at HTB. There, he recounts what happened at the Mumford's place and closes the meeting in prayer. As he does this, he invites the Holy Spirit to fill those present; and again, this has a powerful effect, with several falling to the ground; others working at the church become aware of what is happening and join in. Sandy Millar, vicar of HTB, decides to invite Mumford to speak in their church.
May 29, 1994	Eleanor Mumford speaks at HTB and lead a prayer time, with resulting TB manifestations. The morning service lasts from 11:00 a.m. until 1:30 p.m., while the evening service lasts from 6:30 p.m. until 9:30 p.m.
September 1994	AVC issues a memorandum stating that the TB constitutes a general move of the Spirit, but that restraint should be shown in the promotion of the phenomena associated with it.[22]
February 1995	Bill Johnson of Bethel Church (Redding, CA) visits TAV to experience the TB and is profoundly impacted. He commits himself completely to the movement.[23]
May 24, 1995	Che and Sue Ahn, pastors of the Vineyard Church of Greater Pasadena, see open visions of heavenly things in Mott Auditorium (their church venue). Hilborn writes: "An independent observer, a ministerial student, returning in the church to pick up his car, said that he saw the glory of the Lord in the form of a mist hovering all over the facility and later observed enormous angels everywhere throughout the auditorium. From then on, droves of people

[21]David Hilborn, "The Rise of the Blessing," in *'Toronto' in Perspective: Papers on the New Charismatic Wave of the Mid 1990s* (Cumbria, UK: ACUTE, 2001), 154-156; cf. Read also Bill Jackson's narrative on the history and the Vineyard stance on the TB. See Jackson, *The Quest for the Radical Middle: A History of the Vineyard*, 3828-4184. Kindle.

[22]Hilborn, "The Rise of the Blessing," 185; cf. Jackson, *The Quest for the Radical Middle: A History of the Vineyard*, 4274-4319. Kindle.

[23]Bill Johnson, "Introduction," in Arnott, *Preparing for the Glory*, 7-8.

	began to attend nightly meetings held there by Che Ahn."[24]
1995	John Arnott visits the Ahn's Vineyard of Greater Pasadena, and the church catapults to fame. It soon becomes known as the 'Toronto of Southern California', thanks to its nightly meetings, large conferences, and itinerant pastors who lead events in other locations.[25]
December 1995	John Wimber and AVC Board members inform John Arnott that the Vineyard Association could no longer endorse TAV and its ministry. The Vineyard leadership explains that events and phenomena in TAV meetings fell outside of the Vineyard model. It was said that the AVC did not accept some practices in TB meetings as marks of true spirituality or true renewal. AVC formally separates from TAV.[26]
January 8, 1996	*Christianity Today* releases the news—"Vineyard Severs Ties with 'Toronto Blessing' Church."[27]
January 20, 1996	Toronto Airport Vineyard is renamed Toronto Airport Christian Fellowship (TACF) after Vineyard severs ties.
Transmutation of the TB into Networks of Apostolic/Prophetic Revivalism	
1996	Poloma writes that Arnott forms the Partners in Harvest (PIH), a family of churches and ministries pursuing renewal and revival. for pastors of several churches affected by the TB. Friends in Harvest (FIH) is also formed for those churches and ministries in mainline denominations wishing to affiliate loosely with PIH. "The network is served by 'Family Days'— gatherings held approximately eight times a year at TACF just prior to major renewal conferences and particularly before the annual 'Catch the Fire' event."[28]
1998	When Che Ahn and his church left the AVC, they change their church name from Vineyard of Greater Pasadena to HRock Church (HRC). He then forms Harvest International Ministries (HIM), a fledgling denominational structure.

[24]Jackson, *The Quest for the Radical Middle: A History of the Vineyard*, 4104. Kindle.

[25]Poloma, "A Reconfiguration of Pentecostalism," 108; cf. Che Ahn, *Into the Fire: How You Can Enter Renewal and Catch God's Holy Fire* (Venture, CA: Renew Books, 1998).

[26]Hilborn, "The Spread and Critique of the Blessing," 269-270.

[27]James Beverley, "Vineyard Severs Ties with 'Toronto Blessing' Church," *Christianity Today* 40, no. 1, (January 8, 1996), 66.

[28]Poloma, "A Reconfiguration of Pentecostalism," 106-108.

	When the TB began to wane, HRC's identity shifts from being a "renewal center for the west coast of the United States" to becoming "a new apostolic church." Che Ahn, who was a student of Peter Wagner, slowly becomes known as one of the emerging apostles in the Pauline tradition. [29] Ahn and HIM will eventually become connected to the New Apostolic Reformation (NAR) Movement.[30]
1998	As the TB declined, a new sign begins to sweep among charismatic churches in the form of gold dust. This is the so-called 'Golden Revival', focusing on gold phenomena of one sort or another.[31]
April 2008	The Lakeland Healing Revival or the Florida Outpouring with Todd Bentley begins. This revival has as its emphasis divine healing and miracles, with 30 alleged cases of resurrections from the dead. [32] There were also esoteric manifestations, such as Bentley seeing an angel named Emma putting gold dust on people.[33]
June 2008	Apostolic leaders commission Todd Bentley at Lakeland as an apostle. Wagner, recognized by ministers within their circles as the leading apostle, leads the ceremony, calling it an apostolic alignment. Together with Wagner were Che Ahn (HRock, Pasadena, CA), John Arnott (CTF, Toronto, Ont.), Bill Johnson (Bethel Church, Redding, CA), and Rick Joyner (MorningStar Ministries, Charlotte, NC).[34]
August 2008	Todd Bentley announces that he would divorce his wife and admits to having entered into an unhealthy relationship with a female member of his staff. This leads to the waning and later the ceasing of the outpouring.[35]
2009	TACF changes its name to Catch the Fire (CTF) Toronto.[36] The purpose of the change is to plant more churches around the world that manifest God's

---

[29] Ibid., 108-110.

[30] Geivett and Pivec, *A New Apostolic Reformation: A Biblical Response to a Worldwide Movement*, 216.

[31] Stephen Hunt, "Charismatic Revival and Precarious Charisma: The Florida Healing 'Outpouring,'" *Australian Religion Studies Review* 22, no. 1 (2009), 93.

[32] Hunt, "Charismatic Revival and Precarious Charisma: The Florida Healing 'Outpouring,'" *Journal for the Academic Study of Religion* 22, no. 1 (2009), 84.

[33] Strom quotes Todd Bentley's 2003 article, titled, Angel of the Prophetic. This article is no longer available online. See Strom, *Kundalini Warning*, 65.

[34] Strom, *Kundalini Warning*, 74.

[35] Ibid., 78.

[36] Cartledge, "'Catch the Fire': Revivalist Spirituality from Toronto to Beyond," 230.

	Kingdom on earth and to disperse revival to the nations.[37] "Each of their daughter churches are called CTF followed by the name of their location (e.g. CTF Toronto). Today the CTF network refers to a family of churches and ministries worldwide as a result of the revival in 1994."[38]
2013	Like-minded revivalists in the USA establish a larger, unified network to support each other and promote revival, hosting conferences in various parts of the world. This network, called the Revival Alliance,[39] is made up of six organizations—Bethel Church in Redding, CA (Bill/Beni Johnson), Catch the Fire Ministries in Toronto, Ont. (John/Carol Arnott), Global Awakening in Mechanicsburg, PA (Randy/DeAnne Clark), Global Celebration in Valrico, FL (Georgian/Winnie Banov), HRock Church in Pasadena, CA (Che/Sue Ahn), and Iris Ministries in Redding, CA (Rolland/Heidi Baker).[40] Other revivalists supporting the Alliance are Kris Vallottin, Leif Hetland, and Bob Ekblad.[41] Cartledge explains that "All of these leaders share a conviction that the revival at Toronto in the 1990s has been extended into the present day and has expanded its geographical base. It has led to a post-denominational structure that is fluid and organized around leaders."[42] Because of their passion for revival, prophecy, wonders, and transformation, this Alliance has now been identified as part of NAR.[43]

The historical chronology of this new stream of revivalism shows how it developed from within the P/C Movement, accumulating a hodgepodge of theologies from Pentecostalism's 'empowerment theology' to the Latter-Rain's 'transferable anointing' to Heflin's 'glory realm' and to John Wimber's 'theology of power'.

---

[37]"About," *Catch the Fire*, accessed February 8, 2019, https://catchthefire.com/about (accessed February 8, 2019).

[38]Cartledge, "'Catch the Fire': Revivalist Spirituality from Toronto to Beyond," 231.

[39]Ibid., 220.

[40]Geivett and Pivec, *A New Apostolic Reformation: A Biblical Response to a Worldwide Movement*, 216.

[41]Cartledge, "'Catch the Fire': Revivalist Spirituality from Toronto to Beyond," 220.

[42]Ibid.

[43]Geivett and Pivec, *A New Apostolic Reformation: A Biblical Response to a Worldwide Movement*, 216.

Theological Antecedents of TB Revivalism

Pentecostal Theology to Wimber's Power Theology

Thomas Smail traces the antecedents of this burgeoning renewal theology all the way back to the Protestant Reformation. He writes:

> It is very important to see that the work of the Holy Spirit has been understood and interpreted largely in terms of a particular theological tradition, which stems from the Protestant Reformation, as modified by the Pietist movement and Methodist holiness teaching and latterly by classical Pentecostalism. It was from that very specific matrix that the renewal reached us, and it bears the marks of its origins upon it still.[44]

He then goes on to say that classical Pentecostal theology plays a big role in the theological development of the next waves of renewal.[45] The Pentecostal model views Christian renewal in these two-stages. The first is the coming of Jesus to live as man, to die for our salvation, and to rise again; it starts at Christmas and ends at His ascension. The second is the coming of the Holy Spirit dramatically at Pentecost to empower the Church for its mission, to equip it with His gifts, and to sanctify it with His fruit.[46]

Although this model connects the Cross to the Pentecostal reception of the Spirit, Smail posits that it tends to compartmentalize the salvific work of Jesus on the Cross and the Spirit's subsequent empowerment—the former seen as the 'pardon department', the latter as the 'power department'.[47] If not clarified, this model may point to the gospel of the Cross as merely being the beginning stage of Christianity and the reception of Pentecostal power being the ultimate goal and fullness of the Christian experience. For Smail, this paradigm would endanger P/C

---

[44]Thomas Smail, "The Cross and the Spirit: Toward a Theology of Renewal," in *The Love of Power or the Power of Love: A Careful Assessment of the Problems Within the Charismatic and Word-of-Faith Movements* (Minneapolis, MN: Bethany House Publishers, 1994), 17.
[45]Ibid., 18.
[46]Ibid., 20.
[47]Ibid.

spirituality, writing, "The attendant danger is that contemporary experience [of the Spirit] will be valued more highly than biblical truth, and that what God is doing by His Spirit will be less and less related to what He has once-for-all done for us in His Son."[48] Such would eventually result in a decentralization of the preaching of the Cross during renewal/revival services and a prevalence of anecdotes on spiritual experiences and unusual phenomena.

Smail identifies John Wimber's 'theology of power' as worrisome in this dilemma.[49] Wimber, whose movement is considered as heir of the first wave (Classical Pentecostal) and the second wave (Charismatic), believed that God's power should be demonstrated through the Holy Spirit in the church today.[50] However, he neglected the Pentecostal model of Spirit baptism, opting instead for a model of Spirit-reception upon conversion and affirming that spiritual gifts are given to believers upon conversion so as to continue the present-day ministry of Jesus.[51] His theological terms reflect his acceptance of the Spirit's power (e.g., power evangelism, power encounter, power healing) apart from the spiritual crises-experience of Spirit baptism and tongues as initial evidence.

Unfortunately, this power model is much closer to the Cross-evading theology of power (and glory) that Smail warned P/C believers about, saying:

> An uncritical and unqualified use of power language that easily give the impression that we think God deals with evil in all its forms by unleashing against it a violent onslaught of superior supernatural force, by which it is immediately crushed and subdued. We can use military language in a very naïve way which suggests . . . that all they need is to equip themselves with the supernatural energy and gifts of the Spirit and may then

---

[48]Smail, "The Cross and the Spirit," 20.
[49]Ibid., 26.
[50]Rich Nathan and Ken Wilson, *Empowered Evangelicals: Bringing Together the Best of the Evangelical and Charismatic Worlds* (Ann Arbor, MI: Servant Publications, 1995), 47-48.
[51]Nathan and Wilson, 49; Jackson, *The Quest for the Radical Middle: A History of the Vineyard*, 1378. Kindle.

expect to advance from triumph to triumph in His overwhelming power.[52]

For Smail, this triumphalist mindset is a grave weakness not just in Wimber's but also in the entire P/C empowerment theology. It would ultimately lead to a theological model of power unlike that of Jesus' in the New Testament. Smail both warns of this danger and promotes the centralization of the cross and of Calvary love as essential in a renewal-empowerment theology.[53]

Nevertheless, this theology of power (and glory) already percolates in the Charismatic renewal. Nigel Wright, for instance, connects John Wimber's theological influence to the TB,[54] pointing out that, although spiritual power was not new in P/C circles, Wimber and his network of Vineyard churches reemphasized its use and significance.[55] Wright observed:

> Early visits of the Vineyard teams were characterized by definite outpourings of the Spirit, accompanied by unusual phenomena such as trembling, falling, trances, weeping, unrestrained laughter and the release of anguish and pain in a startling and sometimes frightening fashion. Great emphasis was laid upon healing, the impartation of this gift sometimes being indicated by tingling sensations and warmth in the hands and arms. These occasions were intense, dramatic, and yet, paradoxically, were at the same time restrained . . . there was a great attraction, even to conservative church people, in intense religious experience, actual 'demonstration' of the Spirit, being imparted within a disciplined framework.[56]

---

[52] Smail, "The Cross and the Spirit," 26.

[53] Ibid., 27.

[54] Tom Smail, Andrew Walker, and Nigel Wright, "From 'The Toronto Blessing' to Trinitarian Renewal: A Theological Conversation," in *Charismatic Renewal: The Search for a Theology*, eds. Tom Smail, Andrew Walker, and Nigel Wright (London, UK: Society for Promoting Christian Knowledge, 1995), 152.

[55] Nigel Wright, "Theology of Signs and Wonders," in *The Love of Power or the Power of Love* (London, UK: Bethany House Publishers, 1994), 38.

[56] Nigel Wright, "The Theology and Methodology of 'Signs and Wonders,'" in *Charismatic Renewal*, eds. Smail, Walker and Wright, 71-72.

These scenes in Vineyard meetings are somewhat similar to a TB-type of meeting, revealing a direct parallel between Wimber's theology and practice and that of TB Revivalism's theology and practice. For Wimber and TB proponents, such scenes demonstrate God's power or manifest His presence in the 'in-breaking' kingdom of God.[57] John Arnott particularly believed that the TB was God manifesting His kingdom of love.[58]

Wimber's Power Theology and Latter Rain Restorationism

John Wimber's contribution to the existing stream of revivalism was also noted by David Pawson, who posits that one of those contributions was the idea of charismatic empowerment apart from the vocational context of Spirit baptism in Acts 2.[59] Pawson writes: "Wimber was convinced that the evangelical world would welcome the gifts of the Spirit if they were separated from any 'baptism' in the Spirit (which he himself had never experienced). In this he had considerable success, and as a result of his ministry many evangelicals were happy to be called 'charismatic.'"[60]

However, Wimber's theological stance left believers open to various ways in which they can have spiritual encounters, which Pawson explains like this:

> Denied baptism in the Spirit, the valid hunger for sensate experience of the supernatural was now vulnerable to the offer of sub-biblical experiences, ranging from the banal to the bizarre. It cannot be mere coincidence that the Toronto Airport Fellowship was one of Wimber's congregations, and one of the first to embrace the unusual behavior which made TTB (TB in this study) so controversial.[61]

---

[57] John Arnott, 1308. For a full discussion on the theology of the "already-not yet" kingdom, see George Eldon Ladd, *Theology of the New Testament*, Revised. (Grand Rapids, MI: Wm. B. Eerdmans Publishing Co., 1993).
[58] John Arnott, 28-30.
[59] Pawson, 84.
[60] Ibid.
[61] Ibid.

Moreover, Wimber's disregard of the vocational context of Spirit-empowerment as in Acts 2 led to the view of spiritual encounter as a renewing or restorative experience. The eschatological urgency for last-days witness of the gospel was replaced with the eschatological expectancy of the "restoration of the church to its true apostolic state."[62] This theology developed later as the TB progressed and transmuted (especially after its split from Wimber) and resembles the teachings of the debunked Latter Rain Movement of 1948.[63] The similarities are evidenced by the TB's promotion of the manifestation of God's presence through signs and wonders, the ushering of 'heaven on earth', the restoration of prophetic and apostolic offices, and the concept of a 'transferable anointing' (impartation).[64] Pawson concludes, whether Wimber realized this or not, his "deliberate neglect of Spirit baptism and preference for a model of 'power evangelism', based on the pre-Pentecostal healing and deliverance models of the disciples," were one of the factors that paved the way for this spirituality.[65]

It must be noted though that Wimber wasn't a full-supporter of the TB and the revivalist spirituality. To him, the intensity of manifestations and bizarre phenomena claimed during TB meetings were a bit incredible and somewhat distracting to the goal of discipleship and church planting. Although celebrating the move of God in the TB, he preferred to call the phenomena a renewal, not a revival.[66] Wimber repeatedly asked Arnott and the leaders behind the TB to pastor the renewal meetings so as to ensure it stays Christ-centered and not

---

[62]Ibid., 85.

[63]Hilborn explains that the Latter Rain Movement was a form of Restorationism in Classical Pentecostalism that promoted the idea of "a new band of apostles called the 'Manifest Sons of God,' whose task would be to restore the church to a state of purity and thereby fit it as a spotless bride for the return of her husband, the Messiah. One key facet of this envisaged restoration was the recovery of signs and wonders." See Hilborn, "The Pre-History of the Blessing," 140. The Latter Rain Movement also believed in the impartation of spiritual gifts through the laying on of hands and prophecy. This concept of 'transferable anointing' became one of the reasons the Assemblies of God in North America sanctioned this movement. Although rejected by classical Pentecostals, their theology was later picked up by the House Church Movement in Great Britain in the 1970s and 1980s. House Church leaders like Gerald Coates, Bryn Jones, and Terry Virgo later become prominent in the TB of 1994. See Hilborn, "The Pre-History of the Blessing," 140; cf. S. L. Ware, "Restorationism in Classical Pentecostalism," in *TNIDPCM*, 1020-1021.

[64]Hilborn, "The Pre-History of the Blessing," 140.

[65]Ibid., 84.

[66]Jackson, *The Quest for the Radical Middle: A History of the Vineyard*, 4242. Kindle.

manifestation-centered.[67] He also voiced concern about the lack of orderliness and reminded leaders to follow Paul's model in 1 Corinthians 14,[68] emphasizing from the example of the modern Pentecostal revival that a "revival was never a bless-me club but was a wind that blew them outward."[69] Later, Wimber and the AVC board ousted the Arnotts and the TAV due to the latter's inability to conform to the Vineyard policy.[70]

Ministries/Theologies of Kuhlman, Hinn, Howard-Browne, Friedzon, and Heflin

Wimber wasn't the only theological influence of this revivalist spirituality. Kathryn Kuhlman, Benny Hinn, Claudio Friedzon, Rodney Howard-Browne, and Ruth Ward Heflin also contributed significantly to the spirituality of the TB and the networks that came out of it.

Kathryn Kuhlman was a well-known healing evangelist in the 1960s and 1970s.[71] Although not connected to Classical Pentecostalism and not having a clear healing theology, she was nonetheless accepted within the P/C Movement because of her successful evangelistic-miracle services. She moved in the spiritual gifts of faith, healing, and word of knowledge but did not claim to a Spirit-baptism or tongues-speaking.[72] Kuhlman's meetings were famous for miraculous healings and attendees 'going under the power'.[73]

Israeli-born Benedictus (Benny) Hinn, who followed in Kuhlman's footsteps and her model, gained renown for his evangelistic-healing ministry, which began in Canada.[74] Hilborn chronicles him as being a self-styled, anointed evangelist who claimed to "offer more power (or anointing) to those already baptized in the Spirit and speaking in tongues."[75] John Arnott became friends with Hinn, often going to the latter's meetings to experience a fresh anointing.[76]

---

[67]Ibid., 4225. Kindle.
[68]Ibid., 4225. Kindle.
[69]Ibid., 4242. Kindle.
[70]Ibid., 4499. Kindle.
[71]D. J. Wilson, "Kuhlman, Kathryn," *TNIDPCM*, 826.
[72]Ibid., 827.
[73]Ibid.
[74]G. W. Gohr, "Hinn, Benedictus (Benny)," *TNIDPCM,* 714.
[75]Hilborn, "The Pre-History of the Blessing," 132.
[76]Ibid., 132, 144.

Pentecostal Argentinian revivalist-pastor Claudio Friedzon was a key figure in the Great Argentine Revival of the 1980s. Like Arnott, he too benefited from Benny Hinn's ministry when he claimed to have been revitalized after Hinn prophesied over him in 1992.[77] Following that encounter, Friedzon's meetings became enriched with holy laughter, more people 'going under the power', astonishing healings, drunkenness in the Spirit, deep repentance, and conversions.[78] During the Argentine Revival, his church mushroomed to 4,000 members.[79] He also influenced Arnott when the latter visited Argentina in search of a new anointing.[80]

The ministry of Rodney Howard-Browne, a South-African revivalist in North America, was characterized by holy laughter and spiritual drunkenness,[81] manifestations so prominent in his meetings that he called himself "the Holy Spirit bartender."[82] His theology is predominantly that of the Word-of-Faith Movement (pioneered by Kenneth Hagin, Kenneth Copeland and Gloria Copeland). Hilborn explains that, like Benny Hinn, Howard-Browne stressed the centrality of 'the anointing', which he goes on to define as 'the power of God manifested'—that is, something tangible and capable of transmission through the laying on of hands, blowing upon (see John 20:22), or touching a sanctified handkerchief (see Acts 19:12).[83] (Randy Clark, a Vineyard pastor going through a 'dry season' and searching for fresh anointing, was led to participate in and learn from Howard-Browne's ministry.)

As the TB transmuted in the late 1990s and early 2000, revivalists began reporting radical phenomena like seeing gold dust, gold teeth-filling, entering into 'glory realms', and seeing angels. However, such were not unique to them, for Ruth Ward Heflin had written about her experiences with these same phenomena in her ministry in Jerusalem and in Ashland, Virginia.[84] The product of a Pentecostal upbringing (her

---

[77]Hilborn, "The Pre-History of the Blessing," 142-143.
[78]Riss, "A History," Chapter 2.
[79]Ibid.
[80]Hilborn, "The Pre-History of the Blessing," 146.
[81]Ibid., 133-134.
[82]Julia Duin, "An Evening with Rodney Howard-Browne," *Christian Research Journal* 17, no. 3, 1995, 43.
[83]Ibid., 134.
[84]Her entire testimony and teaching can be read in Heflin, *Glory*.

parents having pioneered Calvary Pentecostal Tabernacle),[85] Heflin founded Mt. Zion Fellowship in Jerusalem and served there 25 years.[86] She is famous for having revival meetings marked with gold dust and for espousing a theology of glory.[87] For her, the term "glory" referred to the manifestation of the presence of God, who is glorious.[88] She emphasized that God is glory; and when His presence comes, His glory also comes (like heaven on earth).[89] However, experiencing God's glory is not instantaneous, but rather like a realm that one enters into through praise and worship. Thus, she called the experience of the manifest presence of God as entering into the 'glory realm;'[90] and once a believer has done so, anything becomes possible."[91]

Heflin's 'The Glory Realm'

Heflin's books reflect her theology of the glory realm. In her first book, *Glory: Experiencing the Atmosphere of Heaven*, she explains that there is a spiritual progression from praise to worship to glory. Her formula is simple—praise until the spirit of worship comes, worship until the glory comes, then stand in the glory.[92] Based on Heflin's book, a deduction of her teachings on the glory realm can be presented as follows:

- If one wants to enter into the glory realm (i.e., the realm of God's manifest presence), one should observe the progression of praise to worship to glory.
- Praise is a gradual increase of emotional energies so as to enter into an experience of the divine. In her terms, praise is the ascendancy or the entering into a state of worship.[93]

---

[85] Renee Deloriea, "Ruth Ward Heflin, Revivalist and Prayer Minister, Dies of Cancer at 60," Charisma, last modified October 31, 2000, https://www.charismamag.com/site-archives/134-peopleevents/people-events/181-ruth-ward-heflin-revivalist-and-prayer-minister-dies-of-cancer-at-60 (accessed February 23, 2019).
[86] Ibid.
[87] Heflin, *Glory*, Introduction.
[88] Ibid., 133.
[89] Ibid.
[90] Ibid., 136.
[91] Ibid., sec. Introduction.
[92] Heflin, *Glory*, sec. Introduction.
[93] Ibid., 9–10.

- Worship is an attitude of the heart, where one expresses adoration, love, and awe for God.[94] It is an experience of becoming more conscious of the quality of divine love.[95] Song of Songs displays this kind of divine romance when one truly worships.[96] Being in a state of worship brings the glory realm.[97]
- The glory realm is a level of consciousness wherein the gloriousness and holiness of God is revealed and made real.[98] With this reification, ministry in the miraculous becomes easy, and anything is possible.[99]
- When a person is in the glory realm, he/she can move in the supernatural. These supernatural phenomena can range from witnessing sparkles of gold, glory clouds, glory sound, angels, supernatural fragrance, supernatural revelation, and the like.[100]
- The way to balance glory realm encounters (e.g., visions, revelation) is to link them to service to the whole Body of Christ.[101]

Heflin's theology of glory promotes the ability to experience God's presence from an abstract concept into a concrete form. This reification happens when a person enters into a level of consciousness—i.e., a state of mind wherein one becomes more conscious of God's holiness, power, and glory. In her term, it is a revelation of God's presence or manifestation of His presence.[102] This reification of divine presence is demonstrated in unusual epi-phenomena, such as hearing glory sounds, ministering with glory clouds, sparkles of gold, etc. The means to enter this state is through an increase of emotional energies that promotes the progression of praise to worship.

It's interesting to note that Heflin's spirituality resembles that of TB revivalist spirituality. Worship-settings become the avenues to enter into

---

[94]Ibid., 119.
[95]Ibid., 145.
[96]Ibid., 110-120.
[97]Ibid., 79.
[98]Ibid., 133-135.
[99]Ibid., 149.
[100]Ibid., 133-192.
[101]Ibid., 197.
[102]Ibid., 133.

a level of consciousness that allows them to reify divine presence.[103] These altered states of consciousness or altered Christian consciousness (ACC), as explained by Dixon, would be "a sense of temporal dropping away so that one becomes more aware of a spiritual dimension of life."[104] In the TB setting, adherents claim that these ACCs are triggered by the direct moving of the Holy Spirit.[105] The current revivalists also espouse that glory manifestations (or unusual signs and wonders) are experienced when God comes in His glory.[106]

Summary

Theologically, this revivalist spirituality has as its historical roots' great movements of the past from classical Pentecostalism to the Latter Rain Movement to the Third Wave Movement of John Wimber. It also has theological antecedents coming from P/C influencers like Kuhlman, Hinn, Howard-Browne, Friedzon, and Heflin. Altogether, one can conclude that, indeed, this revivalism is developed from within the global P/C Movement. In fact, it demonstrates 'that Pentecostalism and Charismatic Christianity is a religion that grows, adapts, and traverses the globe.

---

[103] Hiram Pangilinan, *Presence Driven: The Blessings of Hungering for God's Presence* (Quezon City, Philippines: HG Pangilinan Books Marketing, 2016), 29.
[104] Patrick Dixon, "An Altered Christian Consciousness," in *"Toronto" in Perspective*, ed. Hilborn, 93.
[105] Ibid., 95.
[106] Pangilinan, *Presence Driven*, 194.

Chapter 4

Review of Literature on the Development of the Revivalism in the Philippines

The Pentecostal/Charismatic Movement in the Philippines

The TB revivalist spirituality reached all the way to the Philippines. As in North America, one of the precursors to its development was the explosion of Wimber's power theology. Some P/C missionaries came to the Philippines bringing a message of signs and wonders in ministry, one of those being the late Daniel Tappeiner, a Church of God missionary who had graduated from Fuller Theological Seminary. In 1989, Tappeiner gave a prophetic word to the Church in the Philippines, declaring "a fire of the presence of My Kingdom, a fire of signs and wonders."[1] Then in 1996, he gave this prophesy to Filipino P/C leader Eddie Villanueva—"I call upon you to receive the mantle of Philip. Do as he did. Proclaim My Word boldly and demonstrate it. For I will grant signs and wonders to be done by your hands."[2] Tappeiner believed that the next move of God was to ignite the Philippines to be the "burning bush" of God's glory in Asia.[3]

In his book, *Putting on the Mantle of Philip: Practical Steps to a Ministry of Signs and Wonders*, Tappeiner shared what he described as the prophetic move of God in the Philippines, beginning with the rise of prayer and intercession, then a wave of spiritual warfare, and after that the prophetic move."[4] He posits that these stages were necessary to ignite

---

[1] Daniel A. Tappeiner, "Foreword," in *Signs and Wonders*, ed. Dante Veluz (Quezon City, Philippines: Jesus, the Heart of Missions Team, 1999), xix.
[2] Ibid., "Foreword," xix.
[3] Daniel A. Tappeiner, *The Mantle of Philip: Practical Steps to a Ministry of Signs and Wonders* (Makati City, Philippines: Life Schools of Ministry, 1997), 1.
[4] Ibid.

the Philippines as a sign and a wonder to the nations around it. As such, these historical events were also important precursors that resulted in development of the TB revivalist spirituality in the Philippines.

The Waves of Renewal in the Philippines

1920-1950: First Wave of Pentecostalism

Development of the P/C Movement in the Philippines can be traced in three distinct stages (or 'waves'), the first of which was the coming of Pentecostal missionaries after Protestant missions had already been underway.[5] The first missionaries came for short visits and recognized the need for Pentecostal mission in the Philippines. They were Jennie Brinson Rushim and her husband (Church of God [Cleveland, TN]) in 1918,[6] Joseph Warnick (Church of God) in 1921,[7] and Benjamin and Cordelia Caudle (Assemblies of God) in 1926.[8]

The first Pentecostal church in the Philippines was the United Free Gospel Church, pioneered by Filipino *balikbayans* (i.e., Filipino expatriates who came home), Emerito C. Mariano and Antonio Corpuz.[9] They were aided by Warnick until his death in 1927.[10] Mariano and Corpuz were followed in 1928 by another group of *balikbayans* who had received the Pentecostal blessing in North America and returned to share its message in the Philippines.[11] They included Crispulo Garsulao, Pedro Collado, Benito Acena, Rosendo Alcantara, Eugenio Suede, Esteban

---

[5]Wonsuk Ma, "Philippines," 201; Dynnice Rosanny D. Engcoy, *Pentecostal Pioneer: The Life and Legacy of Rudy Esperanza in the Early Years of the Assemblies of God in the Philippines* (Baguio City, Philippines: APTS Press, 2014), 31-36; Conrado Lumahan, "Facts and Figures," 333-336.

[6]Doreen Alcoran Benavidez, "The Early Years of the Church of God in Northern Luzon (1947-1953): A Historical and Theological Overview," *Asian Journal of Pentecostal Studies* 8, no. 2 (2005), 255.

[7]Allan Anderson, *An Introduction to Pentecostalism*, 2nd ed. (Cambridge, UK: Cambridge University Press, 2014), 191; Conrado Lumahan, "Facts and Figures," 336.

[8]Wonsuk Ma, "Philippines," 201; Dave Johnson, *Led by the Spirit: The History of the American Assemblies of God in the Philippines* (Pasig City, Philippines: ICI Ministries, Inc., 2009), 7-9; Dynnice Rosanny D. Engcoy, *Pentecostal Pioneer*, 40.

[9]Conrado Lumahan, "Facts and Figures," 336.

[10]Lumahan, 336; Doreen G. Alcoran, "The Coming of Pentecostal Fire in the Philippines: A Historical Overview," in *Paper Presentation* (presented at the 11th William W. Menzies Annual Lectureship, Asia Pacific Theological Seminary, Baguio City, Philippines: unpublished, 2003).

[11]Wonsuk Ma, "Philippines," 201; Dave Johnson, *Led by the Spirit*, 9-11.

Lagmay, and Rodrigo Esperanza.[12] By 1940, the Philippine District of the Assemblies of God was formally organized in Pangasinan.[13] Establishment and formation of the Assemblies of God was said to have been a result of Filipino efforts.[14]

Later, other Pentecostal denominations were formed—the Filipino Assemblies of God of the First Born in 1943, the Church of God (Cleveland, TN) World Missions of the Philippines in 1947, and the International Foursquare Gospel in the Philippines in 1949.[15] The United Pentecostal Church (Philippines) Inc. officially began in the 1960s.[16]

1950-1958: Manila Pentecostal Revival

Growth of Pentecostalism in the Philippines (most notably the Assemblies of God) exploded in the 1950s as a result of the Manila Pentecostal Revival, also referred to as the Great Philippine Revival.[17] Arthur Tuggy noted a 500% increase in the Filipino AG membership by 1958, a few years after the said revival.[18] Additionally, Kim Jong Fil noted that this period caused "vigorous religious-spiritual interactions among divergent religious bodies" and resulted in "the emergence of complicated inward-looking churches."[19]

The Manila Pentecostal Revival was part of a worldwide phenomenon called the Healing Revival of 1947-1958, which brought

---

[12]Dynnice Rosanny D. Engcoy, *Pentecostal Pioneer*, 42-43; Ma, "Philippines," 201; Dave Johnson, *Led by the Spirit*, 9-13.

[13]Wonsuk Ma, "Philippines," 201; Dynnice Rosanny D. Engcoy, *Pentecostal Pioneer*, 43-47; Trinidad E. Seleky, "The Organization of the Philippine Assemblies of God and the Role of Early Missionaries," *Asian Journal of Pentecostal Studies* 8, no. 2 (2005), 271-287.

[14]Engcoy, *Pentecostal Pioneer*, 39; Dave Johnson, *Led by the Spirit*, 9-13; Trinidad C. Esperanza, "The Assemblies of God in the Philippines" Ph.D. Dissertation (Pasadena, CA: Fuller Theological Seminary, 1965).

[15]Wonsuk Ma, "Philippines," 202; Conrado Lumahan, "Facts and Figures," 336–339.

[16]Johnny Loye King, "Spirit and Schism."

[17]Kim, "Contemporary Pentecostal Charismatic Movements," i; Lester F. Sumrall, *Modern Manila Miracles* (Springfield, MO: Rev. Clifton E. Erickson, 1954); Luther Jeremiah Oconer, "The Manila Healing Revival and the First Pentecostal Defections in the Methodist Church in the Philippines.," *Pneuma: The Journal of the Society for Pentecostal Studies* 31, no. 1 (March 2009): 66-84; Engcoy, *Pentecostal Pioneer*, 49-50.

[18]Arthur Tuggy, *The Philippine Church: Growth in a Changing Society* (Grand Rapids, MI: William B. Eerdmans Publishing Co., 1971), 151-152; cf. Luther Jeremiah Oconer, "The Manila Healing Revival," 66.

[19]Kim, "Contemporary Pentecostal Charismatic Movements," 3.

global fame to healing revivalists like William Branham, Oral Roberts, T.L. Osborn, Gordon Lindsay, and others.[20] This Western healing revival occurred parallel to, but distinct from, development of the Latter Rain Movement in 1948.[21] Among the North American revivalists who ministered in Manila via large crusades or open-air meetings were A.C. Valdez Jr. in 1952, Clifton Erickson in 1954, Ralph Byrd in 1955, and Oral Roberts in 1956.[22] Luther Oconer noted that these mass salvation-healing revivals became "progenitors of the mass healing movement in the Philippines, which now finds preeminence mostly among Catholic Charismatic groups and indigenous Pentecostal churches in the country (e.g., The El Shaddai).[23]

Late 1950s-Early 1960s: Pentecostals Affecting Protestant Churches

Pentecostals began infiltrating mainstream Protestant churches and even the Roman Catholic Church beginning in the late 50s to early 60s. For instance, the Methodist Church in Manila reportedly lost more than 600 members from 1955-1961 to Pentecostalism.[24] Ruben Candelaria, a Methodist leader and follower of Pentecostalism, explained that this shift (in his case) was due to a hunger for a restoration of the 'lost power'.[25] Pentecostalism provided for Protestants like Candelaria a spirituality that fit their search for a lost divine power. It also laid the groundwork for the coming of the Charismatic wave in the Philippines.

1963-1969: Beginning of the Second Wave of Charismatic Renewal

One of the precursors to the Catholic Charismatic Renewal was the Cursillo Movement, which began in Cebu, Philippines, in 1963.[26] This

---

[20] Oconer, "The Manila Healing Revival," 71.
[21] Richard Riss, "The Latter Rain Movement of 1948," *Pneuma: The Journal of the Society for Pentecostal Studies* 4, no. 1 (1982), 33.
[22] Oconer, "The Manila Healing Revival," 69-71; Engcoy, *Pentecostal Pioneer*, 50.
[23] Ibid., 71.
[24] Ibid., 81; Engcoy, *Pentecostal Pioneer*, 51.
[25] Lester F. Sumrall, *The True Story of Clarita Villanueva: A Seventeen-Year-Old Girl Bitten by Devils in Bilibid Prison, Manila, Philippines* (Manila: Lester F. Sumrall, 1955), 112-113; Oconer, "The Manila Healing Revival," 75.
[26] Purificacion G. Bautista, "The Cursillo Movement: Its Impact on Philippine Society," *Asian Studies* 10, no. 2 (August 1972), 239; Lode Wostyn, "Catholic Charismatics in the Philippines," in *Asian and Pentecostal: The Charismatic Face of Christianity in Asia*, ed. Allan Anderson and Edmond Tang, Regnum Studies in Mission:

movement originated from Spain in 1949 as the Cursillo de Cristianidad (or Little Course in Christianity) and expanded to North America in May 1957.[27] It aimed for the "revivification and intensification of the Christian life of individuals, and through them ... the community."[28]

The Cursillo Movement, among others, was a post-Vatican II phenomena which led the way for the emergence of grassroots renewal movements centered on the gifts and power of the Holy Spirit.[29] In the case of the Philippines, this movement encouraged Catholic lay-people to be theologically discerning and spiritually militant.[30] It also contributed to a spiritual hunger among Filipino Christians who wanted to be in touch with God. Together with the influence of the 1967 Catholic Charismatic Renewal in North America, the Cursillo Movement in the Philippines sparked a wave of interest in prayer and Bible study.[31] In 1969, the archdiocesan Cursillo house in Antipolo, Rizal, was called Pentecost House.[32]

Also, by 1969 the Catholic Charismatic Renewal began to make waves when Bro. Aquinas (FSC), a priest who had a charismatic experience in a prayer meeting in Pecos, New Mexico,[33] started a Bible study in La Salle Greenhills, Manila.[34]

1970-1989: Continued Growth of the Charismatic Renewal

The rise and spread of the Charismatic Renewal in the country continued from 1970 to 1989, when many prayer fellowships and Bible

---

Asian Journal of Pentecostal Studies 3 (Oxford, UK: Regnum Books International; Baguio, Philippines: APTS Press, 2005), 364.
  [27]Bautista, "The Cursillo Movement: Its Impact on Philippine Society," 139.
  [28]Ibid., 234.
  [29]Allan Figueroa Deck, "Where the Laity Flourish," *America: The Jesuit Review* 195, no. 4 (August 2006), https://www.americamagazine.org/issue/580/article/where-laity-flourish (accessed March 6, 2018).
  [30]Bautista, "Cursillo Movement," 243-244.
  [31]Wonsuk Ma, "Doing Theology in the Philippines: A Case of Pentecostal Christianity," *Asian Journal of Pentecostal Studies* 8, no. 2 (July 2005), 217; Dynnice Rosanny D. Engcoy, "A Reflection of a Missionary to the Philippines: Gary A. Denbow Interview," *Asian Journal of Pentecostal Studies* 8, no. 2 (2005), 315-316.
  [32]Bautista R.C., "Cursillo Movement," 242-241.
  [33]Wonsuk Ma, "Philippines," 206; Prospero Covar, "Pagkatao at Paniniwala," in *Reading Popular Culture*, ed. Soledad Reyes (Quezon City, Philippines: Ateneo de Manila, Office of Research and Publication, 1991), 195-196.
  [34]Ibid.

studies began among the urban middle class.³⁵ Two of the more well-known prayer groups were Mother Marie Angela's (of the Assumption Convent Sisters) in San Lorenzo Village, Makati, and the Ligaya ng Panginoon (Joy of the Lord) Community in 1975.³⁶ Timoteo Gener and Wonsuk Ma both recognize that Marie Angela's prayer group, nestled amongst upper and middle class Catholics, was prominent in the rise of the Filipino Catholic Charismatic Renewal (CCR).³⁷ Leonardo Mercado asserts that establishment of the lay-led Ligaya ng Panginoon Community was also prominent in the uprising of the CCR in the Philippines.³⁸

Vatican II's promoting of the apostolate of the laity was a great encouragement for Catholics in the Philippines to pursue a more proactive stance in Bible study and Christian life.³⁹ Many Catholic Charismatics began adopting Protestant terms, such as being 'born again', which refer to regeneration.⁴⁰ Mike Velarde, founder of the mega-ministry, El Shaddai, professed to being a born-again Catholic in 1981.⁴¹

By mid-1970s and into the 1980s, many urban Filipinos started praying for healing, renewal, and spiritual gifts in Charismatic prayer meetings and fellowships.⁴² Later, these prayer fellowships resulted in formation of Catholic charismatic groups like El Shaddai, Couples for

---

³⁵PEW Forum of Religion & Public Life, "Historical Overview of Pentecostalism in the Philippines," *PEW Forum*, last modified October 5, 2006, http://www.pewforum.org/2006/10/05/historical-overview-of-pentecostalism-in-philippines (accessed February 26, 2019).

³⁶Wonsuk Ma, "Philippines," 206; Timoteo Gener, "Evangelicals and Catholics Together?: Issues and Prospects for Dialogue and Common Witness in Lowland Philippines," *Evangelical Review of Theology 33*, no. 3 (2009), 238; "Ligaya Ng Panginoon Covenant Community," *Sangguniang Laiko Ng Pilipinas: CBCP Episcopal Commission on the Laity*, https://www.cbcplaiko.org/members-directory/affiliate-national-lay-organizations/ligaya-ng-panginoon-covenant-community (accessed March 16, 2019); Lode Wostyn, "Catholic Charismatics in the Philippines," 366.

³⁷Wonsuk Ma, "Philippines," 206; Timoteo Gener, "Evangelicals and Catholics Together?: Issues and Prospects for Dialogue and Common Witness in Lowland Philippines," *Evangelical Review* 33, no. 3 (2009), 238.

³⁸Leonardo Mercado, *Christ in the Philippines* (Tacloban, Philippines: Divine Word Publications, 1982); cf. Lode Wostyn, "Catholic Charismatics in the Philippines," 368-369.

³⁹ Wonsuk Ma, "Philippines," 206.

⁴⁰Timoteo Gener, "Evangelicals and Catholics Together?" 237-238; cf. Wonsuk Ma, "Philippines," 206.

⁴¹Timoteo Gener, "Evangelicals and Catholics Together?" 239.

⁴²Wonsuk Ma, "Philippines," 204; idem. "Doing Theology in the Philippines," 217.

Christ, Bukas Loob sa Diyos (Open-Hearted for God) Covenant Community, and others, as well as independent, indigenous Charismatic Protestant churches, including Jesus Is Lord Fellowship (now Jesus Is Lord Church Worldwide), Bread of Life, Asian Christian Charismatic Fellowship, Jesus Reigns Ministries, Word for the World, and many more.[43] In 1983, the Philippines for Jesus Movement), a network of independent Neo-Pentecostals and Charismatic churches, were formed under the leadership of Eddie Villaneuva, founder of the Jesus Is Lord Fellowship.[44]

The 1980s was particularly ripe for the growth and spread of the Charismatic Renewal. Being a decade of political unrest in the Philippines,[45] many Filipinos began uniting with the church in decrying the political evils of the time.[46] In an interview with Dynnice Engcoy, US AG missionary Gary Denbow shared how many Filipinos who were connected to the Cursillo Movement, to other churches, and to the various events in the country at that time, began hungering for more of God.[47] Denbow and Filipino pastor Virgie Cruz were able to establish relationships and conduct Bible studies amongst these seekers, which eventually led to the AG (a classical Pentecostal denomination) being involved in the growing Catholic Charismatic Movement in Manila.[48] Prayer fellowships, Life in the Spirit seminars, and Bible studies became prominent in the mid-1980s to early 1990s, with the classical Pentecostals contributing to the spread of Charismatic Christianity amongst both Protestants and Catholics.

1990-1999: Third Wave of Filipino Neo-Charismatics

If the 1970s-1980s revived prayer and renewal in the Philippines, the impetus in the 1990s was on signs and wonders, deliverance, and spiritual warfare. This was a result of the influence of the Third Wave

---

[43]Wonsuk Ma, "Philippines," 204-207.
[44]David S. Lim, "Indigenous Mission Movement of the Philippines," https://www.academia.edu/12304593/Philippine_Misions_Mobilization_Movement (accessed March 16, 2019).
[45]PEW Forum of Religion & Public Life, "Historical Overview."
[46]Ibid.
[47]Engcoy, "A Reflection of a Missionary to the Philippines: Gary A. Denbow Interview," 315.
[48]Ibid., 316-317.

Movement in North America. This Third Wave (as C. Peter Wagner coined it) was "a movement of non-Charismatic Evangelicals who believed that signs and wonders of the Holy Spirit will accompany the proclamation of the Gospel."[49] Although believing in the continued work of the Holy Spirit, many in the Third Wave preferred not to be identified as Pentecostal or Charismatic, but rather the term Empowered Evangelical.[50] Ma notes that there is no "organization, coalition, or church that may represent the entire third wave movement."[51] Filipino third waver Hiram Pangilinan agrees, saying that Third Wave churches are not uniform in their teachings and that to date there are no networks or umbrella organization for them in the Philippines.[52]

However, some common features do characterize those in the movement. One such feature is the prominence of teachings on power encounters, deliverance, and spiritual warfare, so much so that the 1990s became known as the 'era of spiritual warfare'.[53] Perhaps chief among the era's proponents were Neil T. Anderson, who wrote the book *The Bondage Breaker* (published in 1990);[54] Charles Kraft, who popularized a lower-level deliverance (also known as 'inner healing wherein human emotions became objects of healing)[55] and Peter Wagner, who taught on strategic-level spiritual warfare (or high-level deliverance),[56] posited that this type of warfare was virtually unknown until the 1990s.[57]

Such an emphasis on spiritual warfare trickled into the Philippines, prompting like-minded ministers to write on the same topic. A compendium of these writings was compiled by Dante Veluz in *Signs and Wonders* (published in 1999),[58] which included the following proponents and their key articles or books:

---

[49] Gary McGee and B.A. Pavia, "Wagner, Charles Peter," in *TNIDPCM*, 1181.
[50] Nathan and Wilson, *Empowered Evangelicals*, 12-13.
[51] Wonsuk Ma, "A 'First Waver' Looks at the 'Third Wave'," 190.
[52] Hiram Pangilinan, interview by author, February 27, 2018.
[53] Hiram Pangilinan, "Spiritual Warfare Foundations," in *Signs and Wonders*, ed. Dante Veluz (Quezon City, Philippines: Jesus, the Heart of Missions Team, Inc., 1999), 132.
[54] Neil T. Anderson, *The Bondage Breaker*, Revised and Expanded. (1990; repr. Eugene, OR: Harvest House Publishers, 2019).
[55] Wonsuk Ma, "A 'First Waver' Looks at the 'Third Wave'," 190, 194.
[56] C. Peter Wagner, *Confronting the Powers: How the New Testament Church Experienced the Power of Strategic-Level Spiritual Warfare*, The Prayer Warrior Series (Ventura, CA: Regal Books, 1991); cf. Ma, "A 'First Waver' Looks at the 'Third Wave'," 190.
[57] Ibid., 21.
[58] Veluz, *Signs and Wonders*.

Hiram Pangilinan, having experienced a personal deliverance in 1994 and then ministering deliverance in his church, wrote "Spiritual Warfare Foundations,"[59] an article agreeing with Wagner's three levels of strategic warfare.[60] Arthur V. Gonzales penned the articles, "Inner Healing from Deep Wounds" and "Deliverance from Bondage,"[61] using the research of Charles and Frances Hunter on "Speaking Creative Miracles" to explain the physical wounds that result from deep-level or inner hurts;[62] Gonzales' deliverance strategies differ from Classical Pentecostals in that he promotes 'talking to demons' to speed up the healing and deliverance process.[63] Radziwill F. Santiago, who in 1982 was exposed to teachings regarding back-masking (i.e., backward messages in songs) in the USA, wrote "Exposing the Deeds of Darkness" to warn against subliminal backward messages.[64] His research on the topic was even featured on national TV—ABS-CBN's *Magandang Gabi Bayan* (Good Evening Nation) in 1995.[65]

Also, in 1995, the 'laughing revival', which became prominent in North America, was experienced by Cathedral of Praise (COP), a Pentecostal mega-church of 8,000 at that time.[66] (COP was previously known as Bethel Temple, a church supported by Lester Sumrall.) A year later, David Sumrall, then its current leader, invited Rodney Howard-

---

[59]Pangilinan, "Spiritual Warfare Foundations," 131.
[60]Ibid., 140-142.
[61]Arthur V. Gonzales, "Inner Healing from Deep Wounds," in *Signs and Wonders*, ed. Dante Veluz (Quezon City, Philippines: Jesus, the Heart of Missions Team, Inc., 1999), 151-162; idem, "Deliverance from Bondage," in *Signs and Wonders*, ed. Dante Veluz (Quezon City, Philippines: Jesus, the Heart of Missions Team, Inc., 1999), 165-205.
[62]Arthur V. Gonzales, "Inner Healing from Deep Wounds," in *Signs and Wonders*, ed. Dante Veluz (Quezon City, Philippines: Jesus, the Heart of Missions Team, Inc., 1999), 154; cf. Charles Hunter and Frances Hunter, *Handbook for Healing*, Revised. (1987; repr. New Kensington, PA: Whitaker House, 2001).
[63]Gonzales, "Deliverance," 188-192.
[64]Radziwill Santiago, "Exposing the Deeds of Darkness," in *Signs and Wonders*, ed. Dante Veluz (Quezon City, Philippines: Jesus, the Heart of Missions Team, Inc., 1999), 207-228.
[65]Santiago, 208.
[66]Miguel Que, interview by author, December 30, 2018, transcript, Asia Pacific Research Center, Baguio City, Philippines.

Browne to minister in COP,⁶⁷ the result being an intense manifestation of holy laughter and falling under the power.⁶⁸

Simultaneous to laughing revivals occurring in the urban cities, a new apostolic wave was also rising in the Philippines, likely influenced by the New Apostolic Reformation (NAR) churches in North America.⁶⁹ (NAR is a term referring to a diverse group churches that believe in the restoration of apostolic and prophetic offices in church governance,⁷⁰ as well as the restoration of an apostolic church with signs, wonders, and unprecedented miracles in the last days.⁷¹ Wagner first convened evangelical post-denominational churches in 1996 at Fuller Theological Seminary to introduce the idea of present-day apostles and prophets to the academic community.⁷²)

Since 1992, Dante Veluz and wife Cynthia, who affirmed NAR teachings, had been involved in the apostolic-prophetic ministries, believing that God wanted to restore the five-fold offices in the Church with the essential ones being apostles and prophets.⁷³ By 1999, together with their apostolic-prophetic tandem ministry, they began involving themselves in end-time revivalism with signs and wonders.⁷⁴ Veluz testifies, "We saw the ministry of signs and wonders, coupled with the different prophetic and apostolic anointings [sic], bring tremendous growth in church membership among those who were able to receive the anointing and flow with it."⁷⁵ By the end of the 90s, Veluz and other

---

⁶⁷Revival Ministries International, "Manila Philippines Crusade 1996," Chronicles of Revival: The Ministry of Drs. Rodney and Adonica Howard-Browne, last modified 1996, http://chroniclesofrevival.com/rmi-schedule-1996.htm (accessed February 28, 2019).

⁶⁸Ibid.

⁶⁹NAR churches have been steadily growing since the 1980s in North America. Their teachings are echoes of the debunked Latter Rain Movement in 1948, which was later picked up by Vineyard through the Kansas City Prophets and Mike Bickel's International House of Prayer. By the 1990s, a number of Charismatic churches started forming networks under the apostles and prophets. By 2001, many churches approved of Wagner's claim to a Second Apostolic Age. See Geivett and Pivec, *A New Apostolic Reformation: A Biblical Response to a Worldwide Movement*, 1-8; C. Peter Wagner, *The New Apostolic Churches: Rediscovering the New Testament Model of Leadership and Why It's God's Desire for the Church Today* (Ada, MI: Baker Publishing Group, 2000).

⁷⁰Geivett and Pivec, *A New Apostolic Reformation: A Biblical Response to a Worldwide Movement*, 1.

⁷¹Ibid., 183-193.

⁷²Ibid., 23.

⁷³Veluz, *Signs and Wonders*, 72-73.

⁷⁴Ibid., 73, 98.

⁷⁵Ibid., xxvii.

likeminded churches in the Philippines, heavily promoted this type of ministry, which opened a pathway for TB revivalism to enter into the country's P/C churches.

Review of Pentecostal/Charismatic Literature in the Philippines

By 2000 onward, TB Revivalism steadily grew in the country—without academic study. A review of the related literature in the Philippines supports this observation.

First, Julie Ma's *When the Spirit Meets the Spirits: Pentecostal Ministry Among the Kankana-ey Tribe in the Philippines* was an anthropological case study on the Kankana-ey tribes in Northern Luzon and focused on how Pentecostals interact with the tribal religious beliefs and practices.[76] Her mentee, Dave Johnson, wrote a seminal work, titled *Theology in Context: A Case Study in the Philippines*,[77] the focus of that effort being on the Warays of Visayas Region, Philippines. He discussed the Warays' worldview and religious beliefs in an effort to identify elements that could aid in contextualizing the Gospel to this people group. Ma's and Johnson's researches yielded important information on Filipino spirituality and worldview from the perspective of specific tribal/ethnic groups. However, these works fall short in contributing information on development of a TB revivalist spirituality in the Philippines.

Then there is Katharine Wiegele's Ph.D. dissertation, titled "Transforming Popular Catholicism: The El Shaddai Movement of the Philippines," which used a socio-anthropological framework to describe the popular Catholic Charismatic Movement in the Philippines.[78] Wiegele's central focus was on El Shaddai's prosperity teaching, religious revivalism in the Catholic Charismatic context, and resultant shifts in the religious and political structure of the Philippines. Although useful in understanding the Charismatic Revivalism of Mike Velarde, the

---

[76] Julie C. Ma, *When the Spirits Meets the Spirits: Pentecostal Ministry among the Kankana-ey Tribe in the Philippines,* Studies in the Intercultural/History of Christianity 111 (Frankfurt am Main, Ger,: Peter Lang, 2000).

[77] Dave Johnson, *Theology in Context*, 1-7.

[78] Katharine Leone Wiegele, "Transforming Popular Catholicism: The El Shaddai Movement of the Philippines" Ph.D. Dissertation (University of Illinois, 2002).

movement's theology and practice are not in the same stream as that of TB Revivalism.

Another interesting academic work is Johnny Loye King's Ph.D. dissertation on Oneness Pentecostals, titled "Spirit and Schism: A History of Oneness Pentecostalism in the Philippines."[79] It sheds light on that movement (internally and externally) through the framework of schism and success. Although this study informs as to the often-underestimated Oneness Pentecostals, it too does not discuss much on TB revivalist spirituality or their signs and wonders theology.

The Asian Journal of Pentecostal Studies (AJPS) issue on *Philippines Pentecostalism* provided important discussions of theology, history, contextualization, and missionary reflections on Pentecostalism in the Philippines.[80] Joseph Suico's article, titled "Pentecostalism and Social Change," affirmed the observation that Pentecostalism in the Philippines is more globalized than localized.[81] Suico posits that P/C theological perspectives are merely inherited from North America,[82] which possibly explains the affinity of revivalists in the Philippines to TB Revivalism in North America.

Dynnice Engcoy's interview of Gary Denbow, titled "A Reflection of a Missionary to the Philippines: Gary A. Denbow Interview," is helpful in understanding the historical context of the Catholic Charismatic Renewal in the 1970s-1980s and provides useful information on the contribution of Pentecostalism to Filipino CCR. Additionally, the articles by Doreen Alcoran Benavidez ("The Early Years of the Church of God in Northern Luzon [1947-1953]: A Historical and Theological Overview"), by Trinidad E. Seleky ("The Organization of the Assemblies of God and the Role of Early Missionaries"), and by Conrado Lumahan ("Facts and Figures: A History of the Growth of the Philippines Assemblies of God"), all provide historical and contextual input for development of the P/C Movement in the country. However, they fall short in informing readers on development of TB Revivalism in the Philippines.

---

[79]King, "Spirit and Schism."
[80]Joseph Suico ed., "Philippines Pentecostalism," *Asian Journal of Pentecostal Studies*, 8, no. 2 (2005).
[81]Ibid., 197.
[82]Ibid.

The same goes for the joint publication of Regnum Studies in Mission and AJPS Series 3, titled *Asian and Pentecostal*, which limited discussion on Pentecostals, Charismatics, and Indigenous Charismatic churches in the Philippines. The said series did not discuss the existence of revivalist churches connected to the TB in North America, although it did provide information on the P/C Movement in the country.[83]

Other works on the Filipino P/C Movement include the Th.D. dissertation of Jeong Jae Yong, titled "Filipino Indigenous Spirituality and Pentecostalism in the Philippines: An Investigation into Pentecostal Spirituality,"[84] which showed how Filipino indigenous spirituality added to the formation of a new Filipino Pentecostal spirituality. Yong's main proposition is the utilization of a conceptual tool called "empowered biblical transformation" in understanding Filipino Pentecostalism. His research, together with Jong Fil Kim's Ph.D. dissertation, "Contemporary Pentecostal Charismatic Movements: On a Double-Structured Religious System in Greater Metro Manila," informs Filipino P/Cs about that system in the Philippines; it also confirms the dangers of popular and folk (syncretistic) spirituality if supernatural phenomena are uncritically accepted.[85] Both Yong's and Kim's works enlighten this researcher on the role of indigenous spirituality in the formation of Filipino P/C spirituality. Altogether, their research may be helpful in understanding the implications of TB Revivalism in Filipino religiosity.

Lastly, a two-part publication in the AJPS volume 22, issue 1, titled "Critical Understanding of a Filipino Third Wave Signs and Wonders Theology: A Case Study of Hiram Pangilinan," which the current author wrote, provides needed information on this unique stream of revivalism.[86] Pangilinan is presented in the two-part article as emblematic of the revivalist movement; and his book, *Presence Driven Church* (formerly *What If God Comes?*): *The Blessing of Hungering for God's Presence,"* provides a thorough explanation of revivalism's signs

---

[83] Anderson and Tang, eds. *Asian and Pentecostal.*
[84] Jae Yong Jeong, "Filipino Pentecostal Spirituality."
[85] Jong Fil Kim, "Contemporary Pentecostal Charismatic Movements."
[86] Lora Angeline Embudo-Timenia, "Critical Understanding of a Filipino Third Wave Signs-and-Wonders Theology: A Case Study of Hiram Pangilinan: Part 1," *Asian Journal of Pentecostal Studies* 22, no. 1 (2019), 31-47; idem, "Critical Understanding of a Filipino Third Wave Signs-and-Wonders Theology: A Case Study of Hiram Pangilinan: Part 2," *Asian Journal of Pentecostal Studies* 22, no. 1 (2019), 49-63.

and wonders theology through the lens of a Filipino revivalist.[87] Although unable to trace the historical onset of TB Revivalism in the Philippines, Pangilinan's interview provides important information on the development of the movement in the country.

Review of Filipino Toronto Blessing Revivalists Non-Academic Literature

Despite the lack of academic literature on this particular topic, there are popular and non-academic books written by Filipino TB revivalists in circulation from mid-2000 to today. As mentioned above, Hiram Pangilinan is one such revivalist who has published books on this and other topics. Another is Paul Yadao who published books explaining his perspective on revivalism and signs and wonders.

Review of Pangilinan's Published Works

To date, Hiram Pangilinan has written and published nine books; all are non-academic and aim at reaching the popular masses in an anecdotal format. However, his writing is engaging, expressed in practical language, and infused with testimonies that appeal to lay P/C Christians. Most of his books are in English, although two are written in a mixture of Tagalog (Filipino language) and English.

Pangilinan's first book, initially titled *What If God Comes?*[88] published in 2008, featured his belief in the twelve events that can happen if God's presence manifests (or comes). The book was updated, renamed *Presence Driven: The Blessings of Hungering for God's Presence*, and reprinted in 2016.[89] Both versions contain the same purview that a church should be driven by the desire to encounter God's presence. The next to last chapter of the book contains Pangilinan's explanation on signs and wonders that occur as a result of God's manifest presence.

His second book was on occultism in the Philippines and titled *Hula, Multo, Faith Healing, Atbp.* (Fortune-Telling, Ghosts, Faith Healing,

---

[87]Pangilinan, *Presence Driven,* 220-240.
[88]Pangilinan, *What If God Comes?*
[89]Pangilinan, *Presence Driven.*

Etc.) in 2010.[90] In it, he discusses the various occult practices in the Philippines and how a believer can combat them. He demonstrates insight into the Filipino spirit-worldview and shares a rebuttal on each demonic tool against believers.

Related to his strong belief and practice against the demonic, Pangilinan next wrote and published *Handbook on Deliverance* first in 2012 then expanded and re-published in 2016.[91] It discusses his theology of deliverance and spiritual warfare and provides practical steps to combat demonic strongholds and attacks.

On the topic of healing, Pangilinan wrote two books in 2015 and 2016—*Healing Is Yours* and *Be Healed: A Primer on Healing*[92]—both emphasizing his view that healing is possible because of the atoning work of Jesus. He promotes the purview that all kinds of illness and disease can be healed by Jesus (whom he calls Dr. Jesus) if only believers would accept this truth in faith. The books provide stories and anecdotes to build the reader's faith in the ministry of healing and outline steps to follow in that ministry.

Pangilinan next wrote three books on different topics. One, titled *Game Over: A Closer Look at Video Gaming*, describes his view on the negative effects of video gaming, including the demonic stronghold it can build in a gamer's life. Another book is *Sorry Po (I'm Sorry): Releasing the Power of Forgiveness*, which discusses the necessity, power, and blessing of forgiveness.[93] Written with a study guide (in a mixture-language Tagalog and English), Pangilinan seeks to inculcate the importance of releasing forgiveness, believing that forgiveness can also be God's way of healing inner hurts and turmoil. He then released in 2016 *Discovering Jesus*, in which he explains who Jesus is and how he should be loved by believers.[94]

---

[90]Hiram Pangilinan, *Hula, Multo, Faith Healing, Atbp.: Exposé Ng Occult Sa Pilipinas* (Manila, Philippines: OMF Literature, 2010).

[91]Pangilinan, *Handbook on Deliverance*.

[92]Hiram Pangilinan, *Healing Is Yours* (Quezon City, Philippines: HG Pangilinan Books Marketing, 2016); idem, *Be Healed: A Primer on Healing* (Quezon City, Philippines: HG Pangilinan Books Marketing, 2015).

[93]Hiram Pangilinan, *Sorry Po: Releasing the Power of Forgiveness* (Quezon City, Philippines: HG Pangilinan Books Marketing, 2015).

[94]Hiram Pangilinan, *Discovering Jesus*, Revised. (Quezon City, Philippines: HG Pangilinan Books Marketing, 2015).

Pangilinan's ninth book is titled *Miracle Money*.[95] Here, he describes the miracle of receiving money out of nowhere and shares stories and anecdotes of people who experienced this unusual miracle. His main proposition is that part of God's miraculous work today is the release of money to believers in unprecedented ways.

Of all the books Pangilinan has written, *Presence Driven* provides the clearest explanation on his signs and wonders theology. This work, together with his interviews, allows for the formulation of signs and wonders theology through his lens.

Review of Yadao's Published Works

Paul Yadao has written a book titled *The Mark*, which expounds on his view of God's promise of blessing as a mark over a believer.[96] This 'mark', as he posits, "serve as a seal, a cosmic mark that commands the whole universe to align for our good and for his glory."[97] The book's overall premise is that believers can step into the realm of God's favor and blessing.

Yadao has also co-written with Leif Hetland two books—*Soaking in God's Presence* and *The Ultimate Transformation*.[98] *Soaking in God's Presence* is a manual on the practice of 'soaking prayer'. In it, he and Hetland discuss and provide guidelines on the practice and a lifestyle of meditative or contemplative prayer aimed at resting or tarrying in God's presence.[99] *The Ultimate Transformation* is a training manual for supernatural kingdom living.[100] Here the authors espouse that God is passionate for those who would 'host his presence' and thus demonstrate his supernatural kingdom. As a manual, it is divided into three parts—encounter God's love, experience his life, then express his light. Their main premise is that God wants to bring a literal heaven on earth through his believers.

---

[95] Hiram Pangilinan, *Miracle Money* (Quezon City, Philippines: HG Pangilinan Books Marketing, 2015).

[96] Paul Yadao, *The Mark* (Laguna, Philippines: Destiny Ministries International, 2011).

[97] Ibid., 15.

[98] Paul Yadao and Leif Hetland, *Soaking in God's Presence* (Peachtree, GA: Global Missions Awareness, 2013); Leif Hetland and Paul Yadao, *The Ultimate Transformation* (Peachtree, GA: Global Missions Awareness, 2015).

[99] Yadao and Hetland, *Soaking in God's Presence*, 1-2.

[100] Hetland and Yadao, *The Ultimate Transformation*, 2.

Summary

A review of related literature in the Philippines demonstrates how the P/C movement grew, transmuted and later on accepted TB revivalist spirituality. The available literature also demonstrates that TB spirituality seems to have been precipitated by the influence of ministers impacted by the Third Wave Movement.

Unfortunately, there is a lacuna in existing academic literature in the Philippines. It seems that this narrow stream of revivalism steadily grew from year 2000 and onwards without academic study. Fortunately, on the other hand, a few TB revivalists like Pangilinan and Yadao have published their non-academic literature, which provides us a glimpse into their theology and practice. Nevertheless, further studies from primary sources will be needed to fully trace the development of TB Revivalism's signs and wonders theology in the Filipino context.

Chapter 5

Review of Literature on the Filipino Religious System

The Filipino Religious System

Development of a revivalist spirituality in the Philippines is not surprising in a country whose religious history is composed of a superimposition on ancient traditions and of acculturation. Contemporary Filipino Christianity emerged out of 333 years of Spanish Catholicism and fifty years of American Protestantism. The inherent spirituality of the Filipinos, combined with religious blends from the West, has given rise to some revivalist movements centered on charismatic leaders. The review of socio-religious literature on the Filipino religious system below illuminates how TB revivalism fits into Filipino Christianity.

Pre-Colonial Religious Structure

Pre-Colonial Religion

In chronicling and presenting the Philippine Church, Tuggy explained that, just before the arrival of Spanish colonizers, the Philippines was "a cluster of Malayan cultures and peoples, basically animistic in religion, though somewhat influenced in varying degrees by Hinduism, with a recent incursion of Islam."[1] Generally two pre-colonial tribes already existed in the Philippines—the Negritos (a negroid pigmy people) and the Malayan (migrants from different parts of Southeast Asia)—both of whom observed an unstructured and underdeveloped

---

[1]Tuggy, 25.

animistic religion.² Tuggy believed that the basic concept of this primitive animism was the worship (cult) of the *anito*.³

The *anito* is defined by A. L. Kroeber as "any being which possess the intelligence of a human person and equal or superior facilities but lacks corporeal body."⁴ *Anitos* could be gods or spirits or souls of dead human beings⁵ and were considered as lesser deities or spirit-beings that were more accessible to the pre-colonial Filipino and more active in the affairs of daily human life.⁶ The supreme god, known as *Bathala* or *Laon* or *Kabunian* (depending on the region) was considered as distant and remote, thus the natives would approach *anitos*, which were considered as more reachable.

The widespread belief in *anitos* in pre-colonial times has led some scholars to describe the animistic primeval religion in the Philippines as *anitism* (the veneration of the *anito*), which could be the worship of (1) souls of ancestral spirits, (2) any spirits, (3) beings or non-beings possessed by spirits, and (4) objects made to represent household spirits.⁷ The pre-colonial Filipino family usually had *anitos* in their home altars.⁸

Although popular, the *anito* is an insufficient word to describe the pantheon of gods that each tribe in the country believed in. F. Landa Jocano affirms that there was no dominant religion in the pre-Islamic and pre-Spanish eras of the Philippines, but rather native pantheons.⁹ He lists examples of this pantheon of gods according to regions of the country.¹⁰ For instance, Bathala is the highest ranking god in Luzon, Lumawig the highest ranking in Northern Luzon, Tungkung Langit in Visayas, and Pamulak Manobo for the Manobo tribes in Mindanao.¹¹

---

²Ibid., 21-22.
³Ibid., 22.
⁴A.L. Kroeber, *Peoples of the Philippines* (New York: American Museum of Natural History, 1928), 187; cf. Tuggy, 22.
⁵A.L. Kroeber, *Peoples of the Philippines*, 187.
⁶Rodney L. Henry, *Filipino Spirit World: A Challenge to the Church*, 7.
⁷Jae Yong Jeong, "Filipino Pentecostal Spirituality," 17-18; Stephen K. Hislop, "Anitism: A Survey of Religious Beliefs Native to the Philippines," *Asian Studies* 9, no. 2 (1971), 144.
⁸Jae Yong Jeong, "Filipino Pentecostal Spirituality," 18.
⁹F. Landa Jocano, *Folk Christianity: A Preliminary Study of Conversion and Patterning of Christian Experiences in the Philippines*, Monograph Series 1 (Quezon City, Philippines: Trinity Research Institute, 1981), 4.
¹⁰Some of these deities are no longer worshiped by Filipino tribes today. See Ibid, 5-16.
¹¹Jocano, *Folk Christianity*, 16.

The native acceptance of these deities affirm that, "prior to the coming of Christianity, there existed among the different ethnic groups in the archipelago established belief systems having to do with man's relations with the spirit world."[12] That spirit world was a present reality, for native Filipinos; and rituals were observed for propitiation, manipulation, and thanksgiving by religious leaders—men and women who could 'connect' to these powers.[13]

This belief in a human relationship to the spirit world is linked to the affective significance Filipinos "invest in their relations with nature, material objects, ideas and behavior."[14] In his book *Filipino Worldview: Ethnography of Local Knowledge,* Jocano writes:

> This investment on affective significance is most discernible in their beliefs in the influence of supernatural spirits and psychic forces in their ways of life. Even the concept of nature is replete with reference to the role of supernatural powers—gods, spirits, and life force—in the affairs of man. We call this strong tendency to attribute certain occurrences in life as designed or due to the workings of the environmental spirits and psychic force the teleological dimension of worldview.[15]

The 'teleological dimension of worldview' refers to Filipinos' perception of the man-spirit-psychic force connection.[16] It is central to the dimensions of the Filipino religious worldview.

Filipinos believe that the spirit world is real, powerful, and impactful to their religious and daily life. Nature and the environment too have psychic forces or life forces (*bisa*), which prompted respect and fear amongst tribal people.[17] Trees, stones, fields, and lakes had spirits, and to offend them would result to receiving a curse (*gaba*). Thus, to garner favor from the spirit world and from the universe's psychic force, one had to have faith (*sampalataya*) both in the supernatural powers that

---

[12]Ibid.
[13]Jocano, *Folk Christianity*, 16-17.
[14]F. Landa Jocano, *Filipino Worldview: Ethnography of Local Knowledge*, Anthropology of the Filipino People V (Metro Manila, Philippines: PUNLAD Research House, Inc., 2001), 145.
[15]Ibid.
[16]Ibid., 159.
[17]Jocano, *Filipino Worldview*, 151.

surpassed worldly realities and in the capability of power brokers like spiritual leaders, folk healers, and religious practitioners, who were variously called in the Filipino dictum *babaylans, baylanes,* or *catalanan.*[18]

Pre-Colonial Religious System

As mentioned above, pre-colonial Filipinos believed in a supreme, albeit remote, god who could be reached through lesser gods like *anitos* via prayers, rituals, and faith (*sampalataya*). *Anitos*, which are mostly believed as ancestral spirits, can be either good or bad, bringing favor or disfavor, health or sickness, life or death and can manifest themselves through dreams, visions, and human mediators like diviners.[19] When a ritual must be performed, these human mediators serve as "intercessors or ritual performers with supernatural power, which can be expressed through spiritual trances, speaking in tongues, healing, prophecy, dance, and exorcism."[20]

These religious supernatural experiences observed by tribal Filipinos cannot be easily explained, but it is closely related to what Sunday Aigbe described as an indigenous religious system observed by almost all tribal people.[21] He writes: "The basic concept is that the control and use of power goes from the highest level in the supernatural world down to the lowest level in the natural world . . . in order to have peace, joy, children, rain, health, old age, and many other blessings, there has to be a mutual administration and acquisition of power from the higher order to the lower."[22]

Rituals performed and intercessions made are means of communication between the worlds of the natural and the supernatural. The motivation behind such rituals or prayers is the experience of power

---

[18] John A. Rich, "Religious Acculturation in the Philippines," *Practical Anthropology,* 17, no. 5 (1970): 200; Henry, *Filipino Spirit World: A Challenge to the Church,* 7.
[19] Jae, "Filipino Pentecostal Spirituality," 28.
[20] Ibid., 29.
[21] Sunday Aigbe, "Pentecostal Mission and Tribal People Groups," in *Called and Empowered: Global Mission in Pentecostal Perspective,* ed. Murray A. Dempster, Byron D. Klaus, and Douglas Petersen (Peabody, MA: Hendrickson Publishers, Inc., 1991), 169.
[22] Ibid.

or the need for power.[23] Aigbe terms this indigenous religious system "a power-acquisition syndrome."[24] Such a system, which is present among almost all animistic societies in the world, is said to meet the felt needs of tribal people, the two primary ones which he identifies as being (1) the need for social security and (2) the need for deeper psycho-spiritual commitment.[25]

Need for social security. Tribal people have strong community or group emphasis. The threat of social disintegration is alarming because they hold on to a dyadic paradigm. This makes sense in the Filipino context, since religion in the Philippines is viewed as a family and community affair. Henry affirms that "the family is the center of education and religion;"[26] Jocano also emphasizes that the notion of kinship and family lies at the heart of a Filipino.[27] An example of the connection between family and religion in pre-colonial times was the notion that ancestral spirits interceded with the supreme god on behalf of living family members.[28] These ancestral spirits *(anitos)* were usually worshipped and appeased by living family members to ensure favor and protection. Interestingly, there were no temples of worship in pre-colonial times, because the worship of *anitos* was observed at home.[29]

Need for deeper pscyho-spiritual commitment. Concerning this second felt need, Aigbe writes:

> As we noted, tribal people are beings of rituals and prayer. They place high value on sacred places where they can devotedly commune with their god without interruptions from other gods or people. The less fervent their ritual and prayer and the less sacred the shrine, the less they can commune and acquire power. Just how they can successfully and confidently acquire power constitutes a deep spiritual concern of the tribal people individually and collectively. . . . The witchdoctors, diviners, soothsayers, rain doctors, magicians and other spiritualists and their shrines become indispensable parts of the

---

[23]Ibid.,167.
[24]Ibid.
[25]Ibid., 171.
[26]Henry, *Filipino Spirit World: A Challenge to the Church*, 6.
[27]Jocano, *Filipino Worldview*, 66.
[28]Henry, *Filipino Spirit World: A Challenge to the Church*, 8.
[29]Hislop, "Anitism: A Survey of Religious Beliefs Native to the Philippines," 149.

tribal society. To this end, time is life, for it all depends on how much time a person can afford to spend in communing with the spirits by oneself or through these intermediaries.³⁰

These same observations reflect the deep-seated religiosity of pre-colonial Filipinos. Rituals and prayers were vital parts of religious life in those days. The fear of angering spirits and deities and the worry of not receiving power and favor kept pre-colonial Filipinos engaged in communion with the spirit-world. Jocano calls this desire to be at peace with the spirit world as the desire for harmony.³¹ He writes: "In this context, human existence is understood to be a configuration of harmonious relations between the physical body, the spirit world, and the psychic force that bridges the two . . . To have a harmonious life, one has to follow a precious system of social and linguistic behavior that emphasize man-spirit-psychic force relationships."³²

An example of this deep-seated spirituality among Filipino tribes is the religious practice of the *Kankana-eys*, which are animistic tribes in Northern Luzon that have preserved their religious practice over centuries. Julie Ma writes:

> The Kankana-eys believe that there are many spirits in the skyworld and underworld. They believe that all creatures have spirits, and their spirits join other spirits after death. These spirits intimately interact with people, associating with their lives as if they were living, local resident creatures. . . . The Kankana-eys maintain the belief that these spirits communicate with humans through dreams and mediums. Thus, they seek communication with the spirits by performing rites and rituals. Through the centuries, the Kankana-eys have developed this system as part of their life and thought.³³

Even in the present time, the *Kankana-eys* believe that spirits (especially ancestral spirits) still participate in their daily affairs. They

---

³⁰Aigbe, 171-172.
³¹Jocano, *Filipino Worldview*, 159.
³²Ibid.
³³Julie Ma, *When the Spirit Meets the Spirits*, 103.

feel relieved in knowing that they can approach these spirits for their needs and that they have these spirits with them in their daily lives.

Pre-Colonial Religious Spirituality

Understanding Filipinos' pre-colonial religion and religious system now brings us to agree with Jae Yong Jeong that their indigenous spirituality is about "encountering supernatural power, which has been expressed through religious forms (experiencing Supreme Deity, ancestral spirits and diviners), and is grounded in ritual practices and a recognisable [sic] belief system and cultural values."[34] It's also called a power-acquisition syndrome, wherein the motivation for experiencing the supernatural has something to do with the need for or acquisition of power. Interestingly, the experience of power is not considered dualistic, that is, there is no dichotomy between natural and supernatural. Rather, in this spirituality, supernatural and psychic forces are intertwined in daily life and experienced in an incarnational manner.[35]

An example of this power-acquisition is the process of receiving power for witchcraft, which Dave Johnson described in his book *Theology in Context*.[36] He explained that the *barangans* (people with capacity to inflict a curse, or a *barang*) willingly undergo esoteric experiences to gain higher power.[37] For instance, they talk to the dead or seek the power that was thought to come from mountain spirits or fairies.[38] Once so empowered, these *barangans* can inflict illnesses or curses upon people. This transaction of powers clearly illustrates the indigenous spirituality of encountering the supernatural. It also shows how these powers are used to affect daily living.

---

[34]Jae, "Filipino Pentecostal Spirituality," 33.
[35]Leonardo Mercado, *Inculturation and Filipino Theology*, Asia Pacific Theological Series (Techny, IL: Divine Word Publications, 1992), 48.
[36]Dave Johnson, *Theology in Context*, 59.
[37]Ibid., 60.
[38]Ibid.

Modern Filipino Religious Structures

Roman Catholic Christianity

Christianity was introduced in the Philippines through the efforts of a Roman Catholic Spanish king named Philip II, who sent the Portuguese explorer Ferdinand Magellan around the world. In 1521, Magellan landed on Homonhon (an island near Leyte), conducted the first Catholic mass in Limasawa, and made a blood compact with a native ruler named Rajah Humabon in Cebu.[39] However, Magellan's 'crusade' was short-lived because the Spanish hold over the country was tenuous and colonization was unsuccessful at that time.

The arrival of Miguel Lopez de Legazpi from Mexico City in 1565 began the successful conquest of the archipelago.[40] With him was navigator and missionary Friar Andres de Urdaneta of the Augustinian order.[41] Legaspi and Urdaneta, with the Spanish fleet of soldiers and a few Augustinian priests, brought Spanish colonial rule and Roman Catholic missions into the country. This tandem demonstrated how the Spaniards never separated imperialism from the Catholic mission. In fact, spreading of the Catholic faith became one of the rationalizations for colonialism.[42]

Christianizing the country and establishing Spanish colonial rule were not easy feats, a major challenge being the tribal lifestyle of the natives.[43] The Philippines followed a dispersed *barangay* (village) system of living, with the *barangays* spread throughout the islands. Thus, the few priests and soldiers in the country could not easily exert influence over a vast and widely dispersed people. To overcome this, an *encomienda-reduccion* (entrust-reduction) system was implemented.[44] That system sought to relocate and resettle the natives in villages or towns under the headship of one *encomendero*.[45] This attempt was met with stiff resistance by the natives, who did not want to relocate or leave their

---

[39] Tuggy, 26; cf. Jocano, *Folk Christianity*, 18.
[40] Tuggy, 27; Jocano, *Folk Christianity*, 18.
[41] Tuggy, 27.
[42] Tuggy, 45.
[43] Ibid., 51.
[44] Ibid., 51-52.
[45] Ibid., 51.

ancestral domains. Tuggy notes that "This was the major source of political unrest in the 17th century."[46]

The friars then, following this system, established churches at the center of each *cabeceras* (head or principal town).[47] These *cabecera* churches became the home of the priests as well as the center for religious events like festivals and novenas.[48] The churches, however, were again met with resistance by many of the natives, as Jocano explains: "The initial reaction to this innovation was not favorable. One reason for this resistance was economic: the people were subsistence farmers whose fields were located far from the *cabeceras*. They would rather live near their farms than stay in a far-off village where they could not earn a living."[49]

Recognizing the struggle of the natives, the missionaries decided to compromise by planting in the *sitios* (barrios) small chapels called the *visitas*. These *visitas*, being connected to a *cabecera*, were visited by priests and sometimes trained lay-men for catechism.[50] Thus, the *cabeceras-visitas* pattern was established and became relatively effective in advancing Roman Catholic doctrines and influence.[51] Today this system is better known as the "town church-barrio chapel complex."[52]

Colonization and Christianization of the Philippines steadily progressed under the *cabeceras-visitas* pattern until Spanish rule and Roman Catholicism became entrenched. Although modern Protestant writers have written off the conversion of Filipinos into Catholics as simply due to "the imperializing force of Spain," one cannot overlook the missionary methods that the friars used back then. Tuggy affirms that at the heart of Filipino Christianization was the friars' effectiveness and zealousness.[53] He writes: "These disciplined, dedicated, and often learned men were uniquely fitted for pioneering work."[54]

---

[46]Ibid.
[47]Ibid.
[48]Ibid.
[49]Jocano, *Folk Christianity*, 18.
[50]Ibid.
[51]Ibid.
[52]Tuggy, 53.
[53]Ibid.
[54]Ibid.

Development of Folk Catholicism

Amid the seeming success of Roman Catholic conversion of the Philippines, a quiet but steady development was happening in the Filipino religious system—the co-existence of Catholicism and animism, known as Folk Catholicism. Jaime Bulatao identifies Folk Catholicism as a form of split-level (or two-tiered) Christianity,[55] which he describes as the "co-existence within the same person of two or more thought-and-behavior systems which are inconsistent with each other."[56]

In the case of the Philippines, the logistical constraints of the *cabecera-visitas* complex were one of the causes of this fascinating amalgam of Roman Catholicism and animism. Jocano further explains the development of Folk Catholicism as follows:

> In the *cabecera*, the pomp and pageantry of Roman Catholicism was an effective instrument of indoctrination to the new religion. In the *visita*, on the other hand, such elaborate liturgical symbolisms were seldom emphasized and the people, due mainly to infrequency of contact with missionaries, were less informed about the doctrines of the new religion. This lack of doctrinal knowledge gave rise to a different interpretation of Catholic concepts, symbols, and rites.[57]

There were few priests in those days, and sending them or missionaries into the *visitas* were not as regular as needed. This infrequency of contact resulted in the under-shepherding of a people who were inherently animists. Thus, those people who went to *visita* chapels ended up practicing syncretism—i.e., reinterpreting Catholic rites and concepts to fit into their inherent religious framework.

Jocano explains that this reinterpretation of Catholic concepts is due to Filipino creativity:[58] "The rural Filipino may be uninstructed in Catholic doctrines, yet is not a mere passive recipient of religious ideas.

---

[55] Jaime C. Bulatao, "Split-Level Christianity," *Philippine Sociological Review* XIII, no. 2 (April 1965): 120.
[56] Ibid.
[57] Jocano, *Folk Christianity*, 19.
[58] Ibid., 20.

He is also a creative innovator as attested by the way he selects, modifies, and elaborates those elements he draws from the Catholic church to reinforce the structure of his culturally defined ways of doing."[59]

For instance, the Catholic doctrine and practice of the veneration of saints sits well with the Filipino, because inherent in their religiosity is the idea of a supreme god (who is remote) and of lower deities (the *anito*) whom they could communicate with in supplication for the favor of the supreme god.

In Folk Catholicism, the animistic lower gods were, to some degree, replaced by the Catholic saints. Jocano explains:

> Saints in many rural areas are conceived by the farmers not as Church personalities who have been canonized because of their good work and virtuous living but as supernatural beings with powers similar to those of environmental spirits or the *engkanto*. As supernatural beings, they can be manipulated for personal and group ends. Coercion of saints into giving the devotees what they want are expressed in long novenas, said in church or at home, for a specified number of days, and in elaborate festivals.[60]

Somehow, belief in lower gods overlapped with veneration of saints in the Folk Catholic mindset.

In his field research, Jocano narrates two interesting accounts that exemplify Folk Catholicism. His first story is about how the people in Cebu demanded rain from *Sto. Niño* (a Catholic child saint, often identified as the child Jesus) who was considered as a rain-god. Jocano relates it as follows:

> When there was a desperate need for water and the fields were dry, the people asked [from *Sto. Niño*] for rain and were instantly given it, so the accounts went. Some other times when the rain was not prompt in arriving, the natives brought the image [of *Sto. Niño*] in a procession to the sea and dipped it,

---

[59]Ibid.
[60]Jocano, *Folk Christianity*, 23.

often telling the image that if it did not give them rain immediately, they would leave it there.[61]

In this story, *Sto. Niño* became much like an environmental spirit or lower god of pre-colonial Filipino natives, who could be manipulated through rites or rituals.

Jocano's second account exemplifies what he identifies as a reinterpretation of Catholic rites and prayers into the animistic framework. This narration has as its backdrop the method of catching the *aswang* (a shape-shifting monster in Filipino folklore). The method goes like this:

> In order to catch the *aswang*, one has to prepare three big stones and three big nails. The moment you hear the familiar "tik-tik" or "wak-wak" sounds during the night, start reciting the *Apostle's Creed*. When you reach the part, which says *"ilinansag sa Cruz"* (crucified in the Cross or nailed in the cross) pick up one of the stones and drive one of the nails into the ground. Repeat the process twice. This will cast a spell on the *aswang* and it flies back to where you are sitting. Don't be afraid because by this time it will be as docile as your pet dog. It will alight on one of the stones and wait for whatever you want to do with it. The reason for this is that you have nailed (*linansag*) him in the prayer. You have more power than the *aswang*.[62]

This mixture of magical folklore and Christian prayers for the catching of a legendary monster are representative of Folk Catholicism. Often times, Filipinos in rural areas use Christian rites and prayers to deal with the supernatural, as well as to cope with daily life events. In the back of their minds is the persistent belief that nature has its own life force (*bisa*), thus careful observance of Christian rites and prayers coupled with magical thinking could ensure favor and protection upon them. Jocano concludes that

---

[61] Ibid., 26.
[62] Ibid., 31.

to a certain extent, the environmental spirits [of the pre-colonial Filipino] have been replaced by saints, and the indigenous prayers by the Christian prayers—but the underlying concepts remain intact in that the imperatives of local beliefs and practices still provide the people with proper ritual contexture of economic propositions in seeking the goodwill and assistance of the supernatural.[63]

One of the reasons for the persistence of these underlying animistic concepts is the weak resistance of the Catholic Church against syncretism. Toliver explains: "As was the case in other parts of the world colonized and evangelized by the Spanish, the Roman Catholic church believed that Filipino traditions and folkways could be kept as long as they did not conflict with the teachings of the church."[64] For instance, commenting on Filipino rituals, Jocano quotes a Catholic priest as saying, "These are harmless forms of expressing an individual's religious convictions, of doing his penance, and are therefore permitted."[65] Alhough permitted, such syncretistic rituals are not church-sanctioned.

Lastly, the failure of the Catholic Church to integrate the relevance of its doctrines in people's daily affairs was also a factor in Folk Catholicism. Henry explains: "Filipino animism was more concerned with the practical areas of everyday life. The pre-Spanish animist was much more concerned with agriculture and hunting than he was with his origin and ultimate destiny. Animism was weakest in these areas of higher or ultimate concerns, while it was very strong in areas of everyday living."[66]

---

[63]Ibid., 23.
[64]Ralph Toliver, "Syncretism, A Specter Among Philippine Protestants," *Practical Anthropology* 17, no. 5 (1970), 212.
[65]Jocano, *Folk Christianity*, 33.
[66]Henry, 10.

Henry diagrams the Filipino spirit-world view in this manner:[67]

Figure 1. Henry's Diagram of the Filipino Worldview

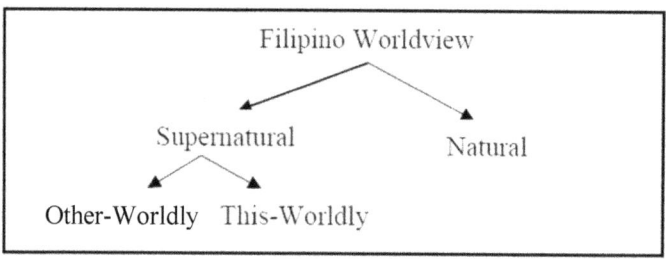

Henry explains that the 'other-worldly' dimension in a Filipino religious worldview has to do with higher or ultimate concerns like salvation, sin, forgiveness, heaven, and hell.[68] The 'this-worldly' dimension, on the other hand, has to do with what affects daily life like spirit-beings, which are concerned with the more practical affairs of this world.[69] He says, "The Roman Catholic Church was given the authority of salvation for the people. The Filipino need only to repent of his past sins and be baptized by the priest in order to have his ultimate concerns (e.g. salvation) taken care of."[70]

Thus, what resulted was a religious system where Filipinos submitted to Catholic teachings on the ultimate concerns but who observed syncretism in their 'this-worldly' or daily life concerns. As a result, Henry posits, "Roman Catholicism had little or nothing to say about the everyday concerns of the Filipino. There was no theology of weather, fishing, hunting, where to build a home, or how to cure a spirit-caused sickness. The Filipino assumed that this was the domain of his own spirit religion."[71]

The failure of the Catholic Church to explain the daily relevance of Christian doctrines and practices, as well as to provide alternatives for the mundane concerns of the common Filipino, resulted in the

---

[67]Ibid, 21.
[68]Henry, 20-21.
[69]Ibid, 21-22.
[70]Ibid., 10.
[71]Ibid., 12.

persistence of a spirit worldview, where spirits and psychic forces still exist and still affect their everyday affairs.

American Protestant Christianity

After 333 years, war broke between Spain and America, and the Philippines was taken over by the latter at the turn of the 20th century. When that happened. Protestant American Christians recognized an open door for evangelism in the country. Arthur Brown quoted Rev. George F. Pentecost who declared to a Presbyterian General Assembly: "We cannot ignore the fact that God has given into our hands, that is, into the hands of American Christians, the Philippine Islands, and there opened a wide door and effectual to their populations and has, by the very guns of our battleships, summoned us to go up and possess the land."[72] Soon after this declaration, Protestant missions began in the Philippines.

It's important to note that North American Protestants were not able to successfully eliminate syncretistic practices in the country, due in part to the blind spots in their worldview. Like the Spanish Catholic missionaries of times past, North American Protestants failed to provide succinct theologies for the daily concerns of the Filipino. While they offered scientific explanations to some superstitious beliefs, their approaches were not able to satisfy the Filipino's inherent need for spiritual connection. Nor were they able to provide a biblical framework that could guide the readjustment of practice and behavior among Filipino Christians.[73]

Western Pentecostalism

The arrival of North American Pentecostal missionaries in the early 1920s brought a kind of theology and spirituality that resonated with Filipinos. Although these missionaries had the same worldview 'limitations,' their empowerment theology and practice of signs and wonders addressed the issue of supernatural power, a chief characteristic of animism. Also, they provided answers to the Filipinos' deepest felt needs, even though not understanding those felt needs.

---

[72] Arthur Judson Brown, *The New Era in the Philippines.* (New York, NY: F.H. Revell Company, 1903), 174.

[73] Jocano, *Folk Christianity,* 62.

The testimony of Ruben Candelaria in the previous section of this chapter is a good example of this. In the 1950s, during the Manila Pentecostal Revival, Candelaria had a Pentecostal experience he described as the "recovery of lost power."[74] Also, the testimonies of Oneness Pentecostal ministers included miracles, prophecies, and healings, which inadvertently contributed to the increase of their following.[75]

A case in point would be the story of Wilde Almeda, founder of Jesus Miracle Crusade International Ministries, the largest Oneness Pentecostal church in the country.[76] Almeda himself experienced a miraculous healing from insomnia, which resulted in his conversion to Classical Pentecostalism.[77] Then from Classical Pentecostalism, he transferred to the Oneness camp and began a ministry of healing and miracles, with emphasis on prayer and fasting.

Almeda demonstrated the relevance of Pentecostal spirituality in the this-worldly affairs of Filipinos in his much-publicized entreaty to the rebel group called *Abu Sayyaf* in 2000. The story (as Johnny Loye King recorded it) is as follows:

> On 23 April 2000, a Filipino Moro group known as Abu Sayyaf abducted 21 people from a Malaysian dive resort in Sipadan and took them to Jolo Island in the Philippines. Thus, began the Sipadan hostage crises. On 1 July, Wilde Almeda and 12 of his members known as prayer warriors went into the Abu Sayyaf camp where the hostages were being held in a widely publicized effort to secure their release through prayer and fasting. Almeda had reportedly gone 40 days without food before arriving at the camp. He and his prayer warriors continued fasting during their time with the Abu Sayyaf, taking only water mixed at times with fruit juices. On 24 July, a press release signed by the Abu Sayyaf commanders stated in part, "The prayer and fasting of

---

[74] Oconer, "The Manila Healing Revival," 75.
[75] A comprehensive discussion of the apostolic roots and the historical development of the UPCI can be read in Johnny Loye King's dissertation. See King, "Spirit and Schism."
[76] King, "Spirit and Schism," 206-211.
[77] King, "Spirit and Schism," 206.

the Jesus Miracle Crusade headed by Evangelist Wilde E. Almeda has pacified us. Their prayer succeeded."[78]

Here we see how Pentecostal spirituality was applicable to the life experiences of the Filipino, even to the extent of believing in supernatural intervention during terrorism crises. This spirituality resonated more with Filipinos. The belief in divine power and the direct relation of the supernatural with the this-worldly affairs of humans speak to the average Filipino.

Summary

The socio-religious exegesis above reveals the inherent tendency of Filipinos to be drawn into mystical and esoteric forms of religiosity because of their roots in animism. Pre-colonial Filipinos had a worldview and religious system that recognized the connection between man, spirit, and psychic forces. As a result, they placed affective significance on human relationship with spiritual forces, believing that the latter affects their daily lives—a belief that was central to the religious dimension of their worldview.

Moreover, there is an inherent power-acquisition syndrome amongst Filipinos, who from the outset were people of ritual and prayers. Religious practices were meant to connect them to higher powers that could meet their need for psycho-spiritual experiences. Manifestations resulting from interactions with those higher powers included spiritual trances, speaking in tongues, healing, prophecy, dance, and exorcism. Hence, indigenous to the Filipino spirituality is the search for an encounter with spiritual powers.

Spanish colonialism, bringing Roman Catholicism, attempted to educate Filipinos in the ultimate concerns of sin, salvation, hell, and eternal life. Catholic missionaries and priests were, to some extent, successful in introducing essential Christian teachings and practices through their *cabeceras-visitas* strategy of evangelism and indoctrination. However, they were not completely successful in removing folk religion. Thus, there remains the persistence of a spirit

---

[78]King, "Spirit and Schism," 209; cf. Sam Smith, *Miracles in Moroland: A Journey of Faith, Love & Courage – The Inside Story of the Sipadan Hostage Crises* (Quezon City, Philippines: Jesus Miracle Crusade International Ministry, 2015), 136, 168.

worldview among Filipino Catholics where spirits and psychic forces still exist and still affects their everyday affairs.

American Protestantism tried to eradicate folk religiosity amongst Filipino Christians but fell short due to the limitations of their own Western worldview. This blind spot resulted in the weak integration of Protestant spirituality into local socio-religious culture. Hence, even after Protestant corrections, there remains within Filipino Christianity a conflict of worldviews.

In the final analysis, P/C spirituality, with its Spirit-empowered theology and manifestation of supernatural encounters, is appealing to the Filipino Christian. It fits their supernatural worldview and is conducive to a spirituality that needs power encounters and deep psycho-spiritual commitment. Taking into consideration this historical and socio-religious exegesis, TB Revivalism, although a narrow stream within the P/C movement yet with its mystical spirituality, esoteric displays, power manifestations, and altered states of Christian consciousness, would prove highly attractive to Filipino Christians.

Synthesis of the Review of Related Literature

The reviews conducted from chapters 2-5 on North American TB Revivalism, on TB Revivalism's historical development within the Filipino P/C Movement, and on the Filipino socio-religious system demonstrate the historical and theological advances that contributed to the formation of TB Revivalism in the Philippines. As discussed above, TB Revivalism is rooted in the global P/C Movement. Its history can be traced all the way back to the Topeka Kansas Revival, down to the Argentine Revival, and later to the Toronto Blessing itself.[79] It belongs to the P/C tradition of revivalism, where methods are utilized to experience revival-like phenomena.

Unlike the Evangelical tradition of revivalism, which was conducted for the reawakening of religion and for mass conversion, TB Revivalism is a more believer-oriented renewalism, with an emphasis on cathartic experiences of peace, love, supernatural phenomena, and spiritual healing. Revival in the TB tradition is viewed as an encounter of God's

---

[79] John Arnott and Carol Arnott, *Preparing for the Glory*, 121.

'manifest presence,' a parlance that was first used by the debunked Latter Rain Movement and later picked up by John Wimber and the AVC. The quest for sensate experiences of the divine is part of the TB spirituality of "search-encounter-transformation."[80] Sub-biblical epi-phenomena, such as seeing gold dust, glory clouds, angel feathers, angels, heavenly gemstones, etc., are accepted by its proponents as normative by-products of encountering God's manifest presence.

TB revivalist spirituality reached the Philippines in the 2000s, right after the rise and spread of the Third Wave Neo-Charismatic Movement in the country. The Third Wave Movement paved the way for TB revivalists in North America to influence Filipino ministers like Pangilinan and Yadao, who, in the mid-2000s, published their own non-academic books. Unfortunately, there is a lacuna in academic literature about this movement. The review of literature shows that academic study on this narrow stream of revivalism in the Filipino setting is lacking.

The need for further research on TB Revivalism is occasioned by the split-level Christianity present in the Philippine's religious structure. Part 4 of this chapter demonstrated that TB revivalist spirituality is superimposed on a religious system rooted in animism. The failure of Catholicism and Protestantism to provide a framework for the relationship of the supernatural to the natural experiences of the Filipino Christian has resulted in a two-tiered religious structure, with Christianity at the upper (surface) level and folk religiosity at the lower (hidden) level. The mystical quality of TB Revivalism is conducive for Filipino P/C believers, whose need for deep psycho-spiritual commitment is high. However, it also poses a risk for syncretism and the danger of forming a folk Pentecostalism.

Suffice it to say, this review of literature shows the transmutation of the global P/C Movement into a narrow stream of revivalist spirituality in the Filipino religious soil, with attendant positive and precarious implications. It gives us a comprehensive historical and socio-religious backdrop for understanding TB Revivalism in the Philippines.

The ensuing step now is to answer the main research question— "What is a TB revivalist theology of signs and wonders from a Filipino

---

[80]Cartledge, "Catch the Fire: Revivalist Spirituality from Toronto to Beyond," 237.

perspective?" A descriptive qualitative method was utilized for this purpose.

Chapter 6

Methodology

The qualitative research paradigm was used in this study for the purpose of "exploring and understanding the meaning individuals or groups ascribe to a social or human problem."[1] In this case, understanding Filipino TB revivalists and their signs and wonders theology was inductively understood from key ministers of revivalism first, before a more deductive interpretation was made. This method is an investigative process whereby the researcher makes sense of a social phenomenon using "emerging questions and procedures, data typically collected in the participants' settings, data analysis inductively building from particular to general themes, and the researcher making interpretations."[2]

Specifically, the research design was qualitative descriptive. This design was appropriate because it allowed for a straightforward understanding and description of an individual, group, or phenomena. Vickie Lambert and Clifton Lambert state, "Qualitative descriptive studies tend to draw from naturalistic inquiry, which purports a commitment to studying something in its natural state to the extent that is possible within the context of the research arena."[3] This straightforward research method focuses on discovering the nature or meaning of certain events. It also chooses its data from a sample considered "rich in information for the purpose of saturating the data."[4]

---

[1] John W. Creswell, *Research Design: Qualitative, Quantitative, and Mixed Methods Approaches*, 4th ed. (London, UK: Sage Publications, Inc., 2014), 4.
[2] Ibid.
[3] Vickie Lambert and Clinton Lambert, "Qualitative Descriptive Research: An Acceptable Design," ed. Pacific Rim International Journal of Nursing Research, *Pacific Rim International Journal of Nursing Research* 16, no. 4 (December 2012), 255.
[4] Ibid.

Since published information on this subject in the Filipino context is lacking, research on at least four TB revivalists, their ministries, and their signs and wonders theology was conducted via interviews.

Data Collection

The data collection strategies of this research design included personal or one-on-one interviews, using open-ended questions. E-mail interviews or messenger interviews were also utilized, since social media today is a fast conduit for gathering information. All of these interviews were transcribed and archived in the Asia Pacific Research Center (APRC) in Baguio City, Philippines. Also, a review of published works, audio-video materials, and social media posts made by the participants in the research was conducted.

Interview Protocol

Conducting interviews is central to this research because it aids in the gathering of rich, qualitative data for understanding the participants' experiences and the meanings they attach to those experiences. To ensure the validity and relevance of the data gathered from interviews, the following protocols were adhered to:

- The interview questions were aligned with the research questions and based on the literature review. Thus, the questions posed to the participants were intentional and necessary for the overall purpose of the study.
- Although the interview questions are aligned with the overall purpose of the research, attention and sensitivity were given to the context shaping the participants' experiences. The questions were then open-ended to facilitate inquiry-based conversation and were framed in simple terms.
- Social rules that apply to ordinary conversation (e.g., nodding, gesturing, actively listening, avoiding interruptions, asking clarifying and transitional questions, asking questions that the participants are comfortable in answering) were observed to facilitate an inquiry-based conversation.

- The participants were encouraged to give feedback on the overall research to ensure the internal validity of the research findings.
- All interviews were transcribed by computer and archived in the Asia Pacific Research Center to be made available for further research.
- The interviews were conducted in English. If the participant answers in Tagalog (our national language) or a mix of Tagalog and English, a translation was provided for English readers.

Data Analysis

The data analysis of qualitative descriptive design is "purely data-derived in that codes are generated in the course of the study."[5] John Creswell illustrates this in Figure 2.

Figure 2. Data Analysis in Qualitative Research

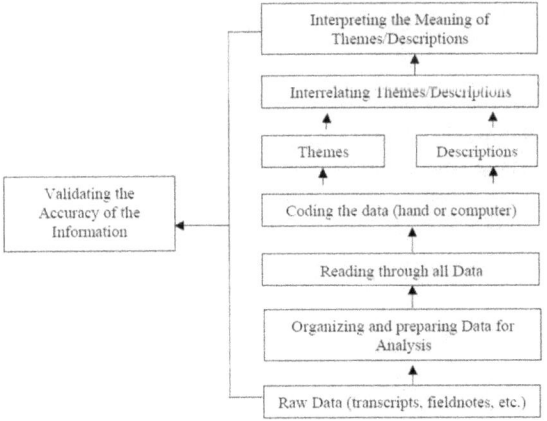

Validation

To ensure internal validity, the data collected were rechecked by the participants themselves. An ongoing dialogue was sought so that interpretations of the participants' reality and meanings guaranteed the

---

[5]Vickie Lambert and Clinton Lambert, 256.

veracity of the data. Triangulation of data (i.e., data gathered from multiple sources to establish themes) were also added to the overall validity.[6]

Information Needed to Answer the Research Questions

To properly describe revivalism's signs and wonders theology, the researcher needed to know the revivalists' views on signs and wonders, their bases for miraculous events, their understanding of the purpose of signs and wonders, and the rationales for their accommodation of supernatural phenomena.

Sources of Information

Books, online articles, sermons, websites, social media blogs/posts, and other available published literature on ministries involved in TB Revivalism in the Philippines, as well as the interviews of four participants, were used as sources for this research.

The key participants included the following Filipino revivalists—Hiram Pangilinan, Apollo 'Paul' Yadao, Miguel Que, and Ronaldo De Asis Betiwan. These four were considered as rich sources of information, having published revivalist books, holding influential positions, having founded revivalism training schools, and being connected to other revivalist ministries. Some of them, like Pangilinan and Yadao, are also connected to North American contemporary revivalist networks, such as Harvest International Ministries, Apostolic Network of Global Awakening, Revival Alliance, and the like.

The information gathered via all the above sources was able to answer the research questions of this study.

---

[6]Creswell, *Research Design*, 201.

Chapter 7

Presentation of Findings

Interview Data of Four Neocharismatic Ministers

Revivalist spirituality resulting from the Toronto Blessing reached the Philippines in the early 2000s. This stream of revivalism in the P/C Movement, however, consists of only a few independent churches having no network or organization to unite them. The following presentation is a result of the interviews conducted with the following four Filipino Neocharismatics who are connected to the TB and its consequential networks and alliances: (1) Hiram G. Pangilinan, (2) Apollo "Paul" Yadao, (3) Miguel Que, and (4) Ronald De Asis Betiwan.

Findings on Filipino Revivalist 1—Hiram G. Pangilinan

Pangilinan's Personal Background

Hiram Grospe Pangilinan is a Third-Wave pastor whose roots were in Methodism before being involved in the P/C Movement. His ministerial education began at Bethel Bible College of the Assemblies of God (BBCAG), where he became connected to Classical Pentecostals. It was one of his brothers, also a Pentecostal, who introduced him to the Asian Christian Charismatic Fellowship (ACCF), an AG Filipino church in Metro Manila, Philippines.

Pangilinan's Ministerial Background

Ministerial Studies. In 1986, Pangilinan left his pre-veterinary studies to pursue a Bachelor of Arts degree in Biblical Studies at

BBCAG. In those days, he became engrossed with revivalism, especially with the writings of Keith Green of Last Days Ministry, Charles Finney, Leonard Ravenhill, and John Wesley. Looking back, he saw his theological roots as being in the revival and holiness persuasion. He finished his bachelor's degree in 1989 and later on would also earn a Master of Divinity degree at Union Theological Seminary, Makati City, Philippines.[1]

Early Years in Ministry. Pangilinan began his pastoral ministry in the Methodist church. However, his affiliation with the Methodists ended in 1994, when he left the denomination to pursue a ministry that was focused more on deliverance and spiritual warfare. With these ministry foci, he pioneered an independent Third-Wave church named Jesus the Lord of Hosts (JLH) in 1999.

Jesus the Lord of Hosts Church to Church So Blessed. As pastor of JLH, Pangilinan's focus was on revival, holiness, deliverance, and spiritual warfare. He continued in that trajectory until 2001, when he became connected with people from North America involved in TB Revivalism.[2] The revivalists he admired included Randy Clark, Bill Johnson, Che Ahn, and Heidi Baker.[3]

Wanting to flow in the same revival streams, Pangilinan participated in a conference of a group of revivalists called the Revival Alliance.[4] He also applied to be a member of Che Ahn's Harvest International Ministry (HIM),[5] one reason being the need for his independent church to be covered by an umbrella organization. In 2006, he was asked to serve as a liaison for Che Ahn, which enabled him to receive assurance of

---

[1] Hiram Pangilinan, interview by author, February 27, 2018, transcript, Asia Pacific Research Center, Baguio City, Philippines.

[2] Pangilinan identifies revival as God's manifest presence and as being in the midst of God's glory. See Hiram G. Pangilinan, *What if God Comes?* (Quezon City, Philippines: Revival Publishing, 2011), 17-20; Reprinted as *Presence-Driven*, 20-24.

[3] Randy Clark, Bill Johnson, and Che Ahn are some of the most famous Third-Wave speakers and leaders in the world. They are part of the Revival Alliance.

[4] Revival Alliance is a network of apostolic and prophetic leaders who come together to promote global and personal revival after the Toronto Blessing. See *Revival Alliance*, http://revivalalliance.com (accessed May 6, 2018).

[5] Harvest International Ministry (HIM) is a worldwide apostolic network of churches in over 60 nations. See "About," *Harvest International Ministry*, http://harvestim.org (accessed May 3, 2018).

membership in HIM.⁶ Later, he changed the name of his church to Church So Blessed (CSB) and embraced TB Revivalism's teachings on signs and wonders in his ministry.⁷

'Winds of Change'. In 2007, Pangilinan joined the Revival Alliance Conference in America where he received prophetic words from conference speakers Jill Austin and James Goll. When Austin laid hands upon him and declared, "Winds of change," Pangilinan fell to the floor and saw visions of himself praying health and healing for people. Later, Goll too prophesied over him saying, "I release upon you anointing for national revival!" Both prophecies were staggering for Pangilinan, yet he received them with gladness.

In 2008, he served as a liaison to globally renowned signs and wonders missionary Heidi Baker.⁸ He rented a coliseum for Baker's Sunday conference then brought her to his church the following day. As she ministered in Pangilinan's church, some members testified to seeing gold dust for the first time.⁹ Seizing upon their curiosity, he encouraged them using Acts 19:11 ("God did extraordinary miracles through Paul"), explaining that mention of the word "extraordinary" served to differentiate common miracles from extraordinary ones. According to Pangilinan, common miracles include those we read about in the Bible, such as healing the blind, mute, and deaf; extraordinary ones are those truly wild and unusual, like instant height increase, gold dust, instant slimming, etc., his sharing the testimonies of Argentinian revivalist Carlos Annacondia as examples of extraordinary miracles.¹⁰

---

⁶Hiram Pangilinan, interview by author, February 27, 2018, transcript, Asia Pacific Research Center, Baguio City, Philippines.

⁷"About," *Church So Blessed International*, accessed May 6, 2018, http://churchsoblessed.org.

⁸Tim Stafford, "Miracles in Mozambique: How Mama Heidi Reaches the Abandoned," Christianity Today, 56, no. 5 (May 18, 2018), https://www.christianitytoday.com/ct/2012/may/miracles-in-mozambique.html (accessed February 23, 2018).

⁹The phenomena of seeing gold dust is much heard of within Neo-Charismatic circles. They say that appearances of gold dust are a sign of God's glorious presence and results in wondrous praise from the people. Ruth Ward Heflin discusses this phenomenon in her book by calling it the 'golden glory,' a visible representation of God's presence. See Heflin, *Glory*, 13.

¹⁰Carlos Annacondia, "Power Evangelism, Argentine Style," in *The Rising Revival: Firsthand Accounts of the Incredible Argentine Revival--and How It Can Spread Throughout the World*, ed. C. Peter Wagner and Pablo C. Deiros (Ventura, CA: Renew Books, 1998), 66-68.

Hearing Pangilinan's message, the church's enthusiasm for unusual miracles was raised to a fever pitch. They started praying for instant height increases during that service, with some members claiming to receiving the said miracle.[11] From then on, he testifies to having entered into the realm of unusual signs and wonders.

Pangilinan's Signs-and-Wonders Theology

In his book, *Presence Driven,* Pangilinan reveals a signs and wonders theology similar to that of Western TB revivalist theology.[12] For him, revival is entering into a flow or a metaphoric river of the Holy Spirit's miraculous working, described as "being in the midst of God's glory."[13] Accordingly, flowing into this river results in acceleration of the Spirit's activities.[14] He writes, "When God comes in His glory, following His glory is a trail of supernatural manifestations. He opens us up to the things of heaven."[15] These supernatural manifestations are what Pangilinan refers to as 'signs and wonders'.[16] Signs he defines as miracles that point people to Jesus, while wonders are the natural products of the supernatural world invading our world.[17]

Suffice it to say, Pangilinan views signs and wonders as supernatural phenomena, which he sees as by-products of God's manifestation in glory and power. Based on his book *Presence Driven*, he believes:

- God cannot be put in a box; therefore, there are unlimited possibilities of signs and wonders.[18] They can be anything as long as it is for God's glory.[19]
- The earthly manifestations of gold dust, gemstones, orbs, angel feathers, and fire are some of the "literal" treasures

---

[11]Hiram Pangilinan, interview by author, February 27, 2018, transcript, Asia Pacific Research Center, Baguio City, Philippines.
[12]Pangilinan, *Presence Driven*, 222-228.
[13]Ibid., 20.
[14]Ibid., 46.
[15]Ibid., 220.
[16]Ibid., 221.
[17]Ibid., 222-223.
[18]Ibid., 232.
[19]Ibid., 237.

believers can encounter in heaven.[20] By experiencing them now, they are experiencing heaven's realities.
- When believers love God, He reciprocates by showing them "heavenly treasures" (i.e., glory manifestations).[21]
- God wants to amaze His people.[22]
- The Church is the "sign-followed" Bride of Christ.[23]
- Believers must be intentional in encountering God's presence; and in that presence, signs and wonders happen.[24]

The summary above, while it only touches the surface of Pangilinan's theology, nevertheless helps us understand the backdrop of his teaching. Obviously, he views signs and wonders to be the expected norm for a church he considers as "presence-driven."[25] That term means a believer or a church utilizes efforts to experience the manifest presence of God, which is reified by supernatural phenomena called signs and wonders or glory manifestations. For Pangilinan being presence-driven is not just encountering the manifestation of divine presence but inhabiting that realm or zone.[26]

Pangilinan's List of Present-Day Signs and Wonders

To give us a further picture of his theology, in Table 4 is a list of phenomena which Pangilinan considers present-day signs and wonders. Although he admits he has not experienced all these signs and wonders himself,[27] he nonetheless cites them because of the testimonies of famous evangelists, missionaries, and revivalists.

---

[20]Ibid., 227-228.
[21]Ibid., 228.
[22]Ibid., 232.
[23]Ibid., 237.
[24]Ibid., 220.
[25]Pangilinan, *Presence Driven*, 20-24.
[26]Ibid.
[27]Hiram Pangilinan, interview by author, February 27, 2018, transcript, Asia Pacific Research Center, Baguio City, Philippines.

Table 4. Pangilinan's List of Present-Day Signs and Wonders[28]

SIGNS AND WONDERS	DESCRIPTION
1. Fire	The fire of God is either felt like a burning sensation during healing, deliverance, or power impartation OR seen as a divine fire swirling around those who have come to worship.
2. Gold Dust	Gold dust from heaven comes in different colors—gold, blue (sapphire), red, and silver. This dust signifies that heaven is colorful.
3. Gemstones	Gemstones from heaven come in different shapes, colors, and sizes. These are mentioned in Revelation 21.
4. Orbs	Orbs are round clouds that appear during worship services, be it in times of preaching or worship. It is believed that these are angels manifesting (sometimes allowing themselves to be caught on camera).
5. Mist	A mist that falls over a believer, much like what Hosea 14:5 described as God manifesting himself like a refreshing mist or dew to his people.
6. Oil	Literal oil flowing from the hands or dripping from the head of God's people. It can also flow from the pulpit, altar, Bible, ceiling, walls, etc. (see Psalm 23:5).
7. Supernatural fragrance	Supernatural fragrance is a smell like no other earthly fragrance—sweet, yet not fruity. It can jump from one person to another or shift from person to person.
8. Supernatural information download	Supernatural information downloads are instances when God just drops into our mind information that we would otherwise not know.

---

[28]Hiram Pangilinan, *Presence Driven: The Blessings of Hungering for God's Presence* (Quezon City, Philippines: HG Pangilinan Books Marketing, 2016), 220-235; idem. *Miracle Money and other Supernatural Provision* (Quezon City, Philippines: HG Pangilinan Books Marketing, 2018).

9. Instant height increase	A person's height miraculously increases an inch or two, even as much as six inches.
10. Limbs grow	Limb growth is a miracle where God creates something from nothing.
11. Gold teeth	Gold teeth received in an instant by those who had lost their permanent teeth. It can also be received as gold fillings. A heavenly gold, it glistens more than earthly gold.
12. Snow	Much like the mist or dew phenomenon, snow suddenly falls where it is impossible to have snow.
13. Manna	Manna from heaven is the same "food of the angels" that God provided the Israelites in the Old Testament.
14. Hair miracles	Hair miracles is where bald people instantly receive hair or those with gray hair receive their original hair color without the use of dyes.
15. Food multiplication	Food multiplication is God's supernatural provision of food, especially in times of ministerial need. The only requirements to receive this miracle is lack and faith in God's ability to provide for that lack.
16. Instant slimming	Instant slimming is where Gods melts away 20, 40, and even 100 pounds of unnecessary fat off of obese people.
17. Raised from the dead	The dead are raised back to life, just like in the Bible.
19. Miracle money	Miracle money is money coming out of nowhere as a result of faith in God's miraculous power.

Pangilinan has also categorized signs and wonders as either "common" or "extraordinary."[29] Common ones have precedence in the Bible (e.g., raising the dead, walking on water, food multiplication, receiving manna from heaven), whereas extraordinary ones have as their basis the testimony of others.[30] The listing in Table 4 shows an admixture of both.

---

[29]Pangilinan, interview by author, February 27, 2018, transcript, Asia Pacific Research Center, Baguio City, Philippines.
[30]Ibid.

Pangilinan believes in the reality of these present-day signs and wonders because, for him, "in an atmosphere of revival . . . the things of heaven can actually manifest on earth."[31] He further holds that the Bible has proof texts for even some of the extraordinary miracles,[32] which he presents in Table 5.

Table 5. Some of Pangilinan's Proof Texts for Extraordinary (Unusual) Signs and Wonders.

PROOF TEXTS	EXPLANATION
Exodus 24:10	God is surrounded by precious gems.
Matthew 6:20	Treasures in heaven can be gems, gold dust, fire, and angel feathers. God is allowing us to have a foretaste while still on earth.
Colossians 2:2-3	When we love Jesus, we love the One in whom is hidden all the treasures of heaven. He returns the favor by loving us back through these treasures, such as gemstones.
Matthew 6:10	When you pray, "Lord let your kingdom come on earth as it is in heaven," you get exactly what you pray for—things of heaven come down to earth.
Revelations 21	We can read of the gemstones in heaven, such as gold, jasper, etc.
2 Corinthians 3:10	God works in "ever-increasing glory." This means that the things God did before He can do again, and we can expect new things and even greater things because His glory is increasing.

Lastly, Pangilinan appeals to John 14:12-14, where Jesus said, *"Very truly I tell you, whoever believes in me will do the works I have been doing, and they will do even greater things than these because I am going to the Father. And I will do whatever you ask in my name, so that*

---

[31]Pangilinan, *What If God Comes,* 200.
[32]Proof texts for Pangilinan are biblical texts that serve as proofs of the possibility of these extraordinary signs and wonders. See Ibid, 152.

the Father may be glorified in the Son. You may ask me for anything in my name, and I will do it." Thus, since Jesus promised that believers would do greater things than He did, then His followers today can go for whatever—for anything—as long as it's done for His glory.[33] In the final analysis, Pangilinan's theology of signs and wonders is founded on the belief that the 'greater things' Jesus promised include even the most unusual of signs and wonders.

Findings on Filipino Revivalist 2—Apollo "Paul" Yadao

Yadao's Personal Background

Apollo Yadao (better known as Paul Yadao), in 1990 while a student at the University of the Philippines-Los Baños (UP-LB), converted to Protestant Christianity through the evangelism of a campus ministry known as Students for Christ (SFC) and soon became part of its core leadership, primarily overseeing the worship ministry. Somewhat later, SFC would become a church called Destiny Ministries International (DMI).

Yadao's Ministerial Background

Students for Christ. As just noted, Yadao's ministerial career began as a student leader of SFC at the UP-LB in charge of its worship ministry. When SFC became DMI, he was named an associate pastor and subsequently became—and still is—its senior pastor. From its inception, SFC had always been a revivalist ministry, the founders being influenced by early revivalists like Charles Finney, John Wesley, Jonathan Edwards, and Evan Roberts. Yadao shares how SFC experienced mighty outpourings of the Holy Spirit from 1990 to 1997, which resulted in many students being impacted for God. He writes, "One of the outcomes of the impact of what God did to us and through us is the significant change in the spiritual climate of our university during that period, from left-leaning to spiritually [sic] awareness."[34]

---

[33] Pangilinan, *Presence Driven*, 207.
[34] Apollo "Paul" Yadao, interview by author, January 20, 2019, transcript, Asia Pacific Research Center, Baguio City, Philippines.

Destiny Ministries International. To date, DMI has 20 daughter churches in the Philippines and abroad. Yadao and DMI envision a "movement partnering with God in transforming individuals, communities, and nations," believing DMI's primary calling as a church is to transform earth with "heaven's influence." By heaven's influence (or influence of the Kingdom of God on earth), he refers to the effect of encountering God's presence, love, power, and glory.

Leif Hetland and Global Missions Awareness. Yadao's journey into TB Revivalism began in May 2006, when he and wife Ahlmira joined Randy Clark's School of Healing at Hosanna Lutheran Church in Lakeville, Minnesota. At a conference there, they both received a "powerful impartation" from Leif Hetland, a revivalist minister and founder of Global Missions Awareness (GMA).[35] Although the couple also heard testimonies from Bill Johnson and his team from Bethel Church (Redding, CA), plus messages on the miraculous and the supernatural from Randy Clark, it was Hetland's message on a believer's identity and the Father's baptism of love that made the biggest impact on them. Yadao claims that this message became a turning point in their lives.

For the couple, meeting and listening to Leif Hetland were a "divine set-up" and an answer to prayer. They had been praying for a spiritual father, and he became that for them. Hetland too recognized the significance of their meeting, writing, "I released a father's blessing to Paul and Ahlmira in 2006, and they said that it had shifted their lives. What I didn't realize was that something was about to shift in my life in a way that I had never dreamed or imagined. I will never be the same as a result of what took place that day."[36]

As a result of that conference, Yadao and DMI were adopted into the spiritual family of Leif Hetland. DMI is officially a member of his GMA, which, in turn, is a member of Clark's Apostolic Network of Global Awakening (ANGA). These two global networks also work in close partnership with Heidi and Roland Baker's IRIS Ministry. In

---

[35]"About," *Global Mission Awareness*, https://globalmissionawareness.com/about (accessed March 6, 2019).

[36]Leif Hetland, "Lighting Fires of Revival," Paul Yadao, https://paulyadao.org (accessed March 1, 2019).

addition, DMI has close associations with other revivalism networks in the world.

Yadao's Revivalist Spirituality

Primary in Yadao's revivalist spirituality is a search or hunger for a divine encounter. This hunger is only satisfied when a believer has an experience of the "manifest presence (or glory) of God." That experiencing of God's manifest presence is somewhat ambiguous and subjective; however, Yadao describes it as "being saturated by God's presence."[37] It can occur in times of worship and soaking prayer[38] and/or as a result of impartation, which he explains as the "supernatural bestowal/transfer of graces, spiritual gifts, and anointing upon one person to another according to God's will and purpose."[39]

Divine encounters, which can happen with or without impartation, are usually accompanied by epi-phenomena, such as face-to-face encounters with God, trance-like states, open visions, and/or displays of weeping, exuberant joy and laughter, shaking, falling under the power, gold dust, gemstones, supernatural fragrance, etc.[40] However, such phenomena are merely incidental, for the main result of encountering God, as Yadao explains, is the "manifestation of heaven on earth wrapped up in one word, 'shalom'—peace, divine order, abundance."[41] He holds that the cathartic experience of shalom or peace is not limited to individuals but can also affect communities, businesses, the government, and other sectors of society.[42]

A cathartic experience of peace, Yadao claims, results in transformation—a change in a person's norm and lifestyle.[43] Part of the transformation is one's 'activation', which he defines as the "use and application of the gifts received, the revelation that unveiles [sic] who we are and what we [are] in Him . . ."[44] With regard to the experience

---

[37] Ibid.
[38] Yadao and Hetland, *Soaking in God's Presence*, 5-7.
[39] Ibid., 5.
[40] Apollo "Paul" Yadao, interview by author, January 20, 2019, transcript, Asia Pacific Research Center, Baguio City, Philippines.
[41] Yadao and Hetland, *Soaking in God's Presence*, 6.
[42] Apollo "Paul" Yadao, interview by author, January 20, 2019, transcript, Asia Pacific Research Center, Baguio City, Philippines.
[43] Ibid.
[44] Ibid.

of signs and wonders, "As we receive impartation, we overflow with more and as we pour out to empty vessels [activation], the miraculous continues and progresses until it becomes the norm and the culture."[45] And since he believes in multiple in-fillings, the search, hunger, and longing for transformative divine encounters will continue, becoming not just a one-time process but a lifestyle.

For Yadao, revival then is a religious experience that can be the norm in daily life. He defines revival as "the awakening of the believers brought about by the manifest presence of God in and amongst his people, leading to deep conviction, repentance, transformation, miracles, deliverance, and freedom."[46] It is also "going back to the normal Jesus-lifestyle in which the supernatural is the natural."[47]

Yadao does not cite any biblical text to support his views on revival; but it can be inferred from his interview that his theology comes from personal experience, as well as from the influence of TB revivalists like Leif Hetland, Randy Clark, and Bill Johnson.

Yadao's Theological Influences

In 2006, Yadao's revivalist theology shifted into a unique form of revivalism, which had roots in the Toronto Blessing. He learned from Hetland, Clark, Johnson, Heidi Baker, Kris Vallotton, David Wagner, Shawn Bolz, and ministers like them whose revivalism can be traced to the TB and the later-formed Revival Alliance. Suffice it to say, Yadao's idea of revival as an encounter with the manifest presence of God and a divine romance between the Father and His children (sometimes accompanied by epi-phenomena like gold dust, gemstones, gold teeth, etc.) became part of his theology and spirituality by 2006 and onward.

Yadao's Signs and Wonders Theology

Description and Rationale. Yadao's revivalist spirituality is directly connected to his signs and wonders theology. Supernatural

---

[45]Ibid.
[46]Ibid., 3.
[47]Ibid.

manifestations that show up when God's glory comes in a revival meeting are what he describes as signs and wonders.[48] Specifically, he defines them as "miraculous acts of God that demonstrate his power and the supremacy of his kingdom, addressing the needs of men through supernatural means, and [they] are humanly impossible."[49] Yadao didn't give an exhaustive list of signs and wonders in his interview. Instead, he wrote some of them down, which are listed in Table 6.[50] (Although not exhaustive, he claims that these supernatural manifestations occur when God's glory manifests.)

Table 6. Yadao's Sample List of Signs and Wonders.

No.	SAMPLE LIST OF SIGNS AND WONDERS
1.	All sorts of supernatural healing (e.g., blind eyes opened, the lame walking, the mute speaking)
2.	Deliverance
3.	Miraculous provisions (e.g., multiplication of bread/food, supernatural provision)
4.	Angelic manifestations
5.	Gold dust
6.	Fire
7.	Gemstones
8.	Oil (which he claims sometimes come out of his hands while praying for someone)
9.	Manna showing up
10.	Mist/fog
11.	Raindrops
12.	Supernatural fragrance

In talking about God's glory, Yadao defines it as "the summation of all that God has (power, authority, wisdom, creativity, etc.) and all that God is (holy, love, righteous, almighty, beauty)."[51] For him, when God's glory becomes real and tangible in an assembly, any supernatural manifestation can show up. Unlike Pangilinan, he doesn't differentiate

---

[48] Apollo "Paul" Yadao, interview by author, January 20, 2019, transcript, Asia Pacific Research Center, Baguio City, Philippines.
[49] Ibid.
[50] Ibid.
[51] Ibid.

between ordinary (i.e., manifestations with biblical precedence) or extraordinary (i.e., manifestations without biblical precedence) signs and wonders.

Yadao doesn't provide specific biblical rationale for each manifestation, but rather give an overall rationale for the claims that these signs and wonders occur today. He offers as proof texts Mark 16:15-18, Matthew 10:7-8, and John 14:12.[52] Based on these verses, he believes that the manifestation of signs and wonders are connected to the proclamation of the Gospel (Mark 16:15-18), to the reality of the presence of God's kingdom (Matthew 10:7-8), and to the 'greater works'" Jesus promised that His followers will do (John 14:12).

Yadao further explains his belief in signs and wonders as part of being in the new covenant of Jesus. He writes:

> It was stated nowhere in the Bible that signs and wonders and the miraculous will cease to operate in our time or dispensation. Having received total forgiveness and being born again into the Kingdom of God as sons and daughters of God through the Blood of Jesus, we belong to the New Covenant that has long replaced the Old Covenant that was inferior and had to be done away with through the perfect sacrifice of Jesus. In short, how can we who are under the Blood of the Lamb obtain lesser promises when what we have is the perfect once-for-all sacrifice while the Old Covenant settles for animal sacrifice which was just a representation of what is to come.[53]

Hence, for him, in being part of the New Covenant, believers should expect the greater things and the fulfillment of better promises from the Lord. While, of course, Jesus remains the model of a ministry in signs and wonders, Yadao claims that believers ought to continue His supernatural life and ministry in this age.

---

[52]Ibid.

[53]Apollo "Paul" Yadao, interview by author, January 20, 2019, transcript, Asia Pacific Research Center, Baguio City, Philippines.

Purposes and Experiences of Signs and Wonders. As to the purposes for signs and wonders in the ministry today, Yadao lists five as follow:

- They serve as signals to the reality of a supernatural God.
- They point people to know who God is.
- They awaken awareness and sensitivity to God's world.[54]
- They demonstrate how God's world is superior to the material world.[55]
- They are God's self-revelation and an expression of His goodness to His creation."[56]

As to what one needs to do to experience these signs and wonders for ministry, Yadao offers to following four tips:

- Cultivate intimacy with God (John 15:5).
- Have a faith that's bold enough to pursue a life of and ministry in signs and wonders. (He says, "Signs and wonders follow those who believe.[57] However, the context of this statement does not reflect that of Mark 16:15-20, but rather the TB revivalist's belief that signs and wonders follow those who believe in the possibility and reality of a supernatural lifestyle on earth.[58] This is the type of faith Yadao also promotes—one that earnestly and boldly expects, is always hungry for signs and wonders, and makes room for God's presence and glory.[59])
- Be motivated to minister with compassion and to demonstrate the loving heart of God.[60]

---

[54]Ibid.
[55]Ibid.
[56]Ibid.
[57]Ibid.
[58]Yadao's explanation did not include the overall context of Mark 16:15-20—i.e., signs followed preaching of the Gospel. It is crucial to see that the Gospel of Mark doesn't say that signs and wonders follow those who believe in signs and wonders, but instead that signs and wonders follow those who believe Jesus and proclaim His Gospel.
[59]Apollo "Paul" Yadao, interview by author, January 20, 2019, transcript, Asia Pacific Research Center, Baguio City, Philippines.
[60]Apollo "Paul" Yadao, interview by author, January 20, 2019, transcript, Asia Pacific Research Center, Baguio City, Philippines.

- Seek declaration and revelation of a prophetic word, prayer, testimonies, and word of knowledge.[61]

Yadao shared how his experience of signs and wonders became more pronounced after he received an impartation from Leif Hetland in 2006. In testifying to having witnessed numerous healing, deliverance, and supernatural manifestations,"[62] he writes,

> To name some of the healings we witnessed- blind eyes healed, lame men walking, people getting out wheelchairs, tumors dissolved, confirmed healing from cancer, bone alignments, the disappearance of scars in the body, deaf ears open, deliverance from witchcraft, demonic possession and many more. Some supernatural signs: strong angelic presence, feathers showing up from out of nowhere, gemstones appearance, sometimes there's oil in my hands as I pray for people and the like [sic].[63]

His experiences were usually in the context of crusades, conferences, and leadership training in areas like Pakistan, India, and other countries in southeast Asia.[64]

Discerning Signs and Wonders. Yadao recognizes that revival meetings are a mixed brew of the divine and the flesh. Thus, he affirms the importance of evaluating what's from God and what's from the flesh. He explains that the Bible, being the Word of God, remains the plumb line for people's religious experiences. He also checks to see if a given manifestation glorifies God or people, points to Jesus or to a different direction, and transforms believers into Christlikeness. Further, he appeals to the 'fruit principle'—i.e., a manifestation is known to be of God or not based on the fruit it produces.

---

[61] Ibid.
[62] Ibid.
[63] Ibid.
[64] Ibid.

Toronto Blessing Revivalism in the Philippines

Although Yadao cannot pinpoint the exact time TB Revivalism began in the Philippines, he holds that it entered the country via "an ever-increasing build-up of momentum."[65] For him, religious waves, such as the prophetic, prayer movements, and restoration of apostolic ministries in the country contributed to the build-up. He also believes that this type of revivalism is a "unique expression of revival" in the Philippines which occurs parallel to the redemption of Filipino culture and fulfillment of the country's destiny as a nation.[66]

Findings on Filipino Revivalist 3—Miguel Que

Que's Personal Background

Miguel Que is the founder and pastor of a revivalist ministry called Freshwind Global Ministries. He was converted to Protestant Christianity as a student at Hope Christian High School. His father was a Catholic, while his mother was non-religious. Que himself claims to have not been a Catholic but was positively impacted by Evangelicalism while in high school. Although initially mentored by Southern Baptists and Presbyterians, he felt that these denominations lacked the supernatural power described in the Bible. So he sought for that power in life and ministry, eventually finding it in Pentecostal and Charismatic ministries. He began watching 700 Club television programs and reading Kenneth Hagin's books. In 1985, he entered the fold of a Pentecostal church—the Cathedral of Praise (COP) in Metro Manila, Philippines.

Que's Ministerial Background

Cathedral of Praise. Que's ministerial career began as an associate pastor of COP from 1995-2001. His involvement there included youth ministry, pastoral care, and administrator for COP's Bible college. Que shares how the 'laughing revival' hit COP in 1995. This was a year before Rodney Howard-Browne came to the Philippines to conduct

---

[65]Ibid.
[66]Ibid.

revivals with manifestations of laughter and 'falling under the power.'[67] Que also started moving in the gift of healing while serving as youth department head.

Itinerant Revivalist Ministry. Sensing a call towards a supernatural revivalist ministry, Que resigned from his position at COP in 2001 to become an itinerant revivalist. By 2005, his ministry began displaying 'glory manifestations', such as gold dust, trances, instant height increase, etc. In 2012, he joined Hiram Pangilinan's Church So Blessed, recognizing that he moved in the same spirituality with the said church.

Freshwind Global Ministries. As an itinerant revivalist, Que's ministry in churches began displaying manifestations of what he called 'signs and wonders'; the worship and ministering times also manifested revival-like experiences. This resulted in him often being invited to conduct revival services. Que explains that revival occurs when the 'manifest presence of God' saturates believers. During these moments, believers have an increased awareness of God's presence and power, which also results in the restoration of holiness and passionate love for God.

Initially, the churches Que ministered to did not know how to sustain the revivalist spirituality for long periods of time. So he began building relationships with pastors of different churches. Soon, those he fellowshipped with likewise began seeing signs and wonders occurring in their ministries. These fruitful relationships resulted in Que founding Freshwind Global Ministries (FGM) in 2007. He describes FGM as "a network of ministers, churches, and ministries who are passionate about creating cultures of God's love, wisdom, and power."[68]

Impart Supernatural School. Que also claims to have received a vision from Jesus,[69] in which Jesus told him, "You are doing it all wrong. I want you to do training, not just informal bonding."[70] The result of that vision was the formation of a school called Impart Supernatural School (ISS). Being an arm of FGM, it is a training school for revivalism and moving in signs and wonders. Que organizes meetings in churches

---

[67] Revival Ministries International, "Manila Philippines Crusade 1996."
[68] Miguel Que, interview by author, December 30, 2018, transcript, Asia Pacific Research Center, Baguio City, Philippines.
[69] Ibid.
[70] Ibid.

located in northern Metro Manila; also a regular non-church host meeting for ISS is conducted every Sunday at 11F King's Court, Chino Roces Avenue, Makati City, Philippines.

Que's Theological Influences

Pentecostal and Charismatic theology left a big impact on Que. The P/C belief in continuation of the Holy Spirit's supernatural work in the world today is something that he adheres to. Moreover, from his involvement with Classical Pentecostals, he still believes in a second crisis experience of Spirit-baptism. He also holds that a believer should have multiple infillings of the Spirit, using John 7:37, Acts 13:52, Ephesians 5:18, and Galatians 3:5 as biblical bases.[71] However, unlike Classical Pentecostals, Que doesn't adhere to the doctrine of speaking in tongues as initial evidence, but rather believes that the evidence of Spirit baptism is power. Currently, he considers himself to be an independent Charismatic.

Que's journey into P/C spirituality eventually led him to a revivalist spirituality connected to North American TB Revivalism. Some of the ministers whose theology he agrees with include: Bill Johnson, Todd Bentley, Jack Deere, Heidi Baker, Shawn Bolz, and Randy Clark; and he also claims to flow in the same spirituality as Hiram Pangilinan.

Que's Theology of Signs and Wonders

Description. Que believes that signs and wonders are extraordinary miracles that point to Jesus.[72] These manifestations are possible because Jesus is the miracle worker who is alive today and who promises to always be with His followers. Like other TB revivalists, Que also believes that there is no limit to what God can do. So signs and wonders can be anything. He bases his claims on John 14:12, where Jesus promised 'greater things' for His believers.

The ability to minister greater things, which can include unprecedented signs and wonders, comes from God. This anointing can come *indirectly* from the Lord through impartation. (Que defines

---

[71]Miguel Que, interview by author, December 30, 2018, transcript, Asia Pacific Research Center, Baguio City, Philippines.

[72]Ibid.

impartation as the transfer of supernatural gifts by the laying on of hands;[73] and his belief as to impartation is based on 2 Timothy 1:6.) Signs and wonders can also come *directly* from the Lord as believers put themselves in a posture to receive the empowerment. Table 7 lists the actions that Que suggests postures oneself to flowing in signs and wonders.[74]

Table 7. Que's Suggested Tips for Flowing in Signs and Wonders

POSTURING	SUPPORTING VERSE
1. Earnestly desire life and ministry with signs and wonders	1 Corinthians 14:1
2. Cultivate a faith that acts	James 2:17
3. Have confidence before the throne of God (i.e., before his presence)	Hebrews 4:16
4. Abide in Christ	John 15:5
5. Be filled with the Holy Spirit	Acts 1:9

Purpose. Que believes that signs and wonders occur today because they are part of the proclamation of the Gospel, arguing that "Demonstration-less gospel preaching is unheard of in the Bible."[75] He also believes that God uses signs and wonders to lead people (even the stubborn ones) into faith and to fill them with awe. Moreover, he claims that believers who are full of God's grace and power are expected to overflow in signs and wonders. And he further believes that God uses signs and wonders to strengthen Christians.

Some Present-Day Signs and Wonders. Believing in the infinite ways that God can move, Que shares a sample list of signs and wonders in Table 8. This list doesn't put God in a box; it simply serves to enumerate some of the manifestations he claims to have personally witnessed.

---

[73]Ibid.
[74]Ibid.
[75]Miguel Que, interview by author, December 30, 2018, transcript, Asia Pacific Research Center, Baguio City, Philippines.

Table 8. Que's Sample List of Signs and Wonders.

Gifts of the Spirit: *(1 Corinthians 12)* Word of wisdom Word of knowledge Discerning of spirit Prophesy Interpretation of tongues Gift of Faith Working of miracles Gifts of healings	*Signs of Heaven* Gemstones. (Exodus 39: 10-14) Feathers. (Psalm 91:4) Gold dust. (Psalm 68:13) Supernatural in pictures. Oil. (Psalm 23:5) Cloud of glory. (1 Kings 8:11)
Materialization Food multiplication. (John 6:10) Money materializing Translocation (Acts 8:39)	*Love tokens (Matthew 21:22)* Instant weight change (increase or lost) Instant height increase Instant hair growth
Spirit-Inspired Manifestations Laughing in the Spirit. (Job 8:21) Dancing in the Spirit. (Zephaniah 3:17) Running In the Spirit. (1 Kings 18:46) Jumping in the Spirit. (2 Samuel 2:12) Shaking in the Spirit. (Dan. 10:10)	*Opening of Spiritual Sense* Seeing. (2 King 6:17) Hearing Feeling (1 Samuel 10:8) Tasting (Revelation 10:9) Smelling (Songs of Solomon 1:3) Spiritual trances/ travels (Ezekiel 8:3)

Discerning Signs and Wonders. In evaluating supernatural manifestations, Que adheres to the 'fruit principle.' He writes: "The devil can speak to people and also give false visions. The devil can turn sticks into snakes like [sic] Moses did. The devil can counterfeit most miracles God does; therefore, we don't discern the tree by its stem but by its fruit."[76]

---

[76]Miguel Que, interview by author, December 30, 2018, transcript, Asia Pacific Research Center, Baguio City, Philippines.

Que believes that the experience of signs and wonders should lead to the strengthening of God's word and works in the world, not mislead people from God's character and word. The Word of God must validate prophetic revelation and must remain as the backbone of every believer. He cites the use of historic-grammatical interpretation—i.e., going back to authorial intent in interpreting Scripture—as important in avoiding deceptive signs and wonders.

Findings on Filipino Revivalist 4—Ronald De Asis Betiwan

Betiwan's Personal Background

Ronald De Asis Betiwan is the pastor of an independent Third-Wave church named NET Missions Fellowship Church in Iligan City, Mindanao, Philippines. In 1995, he converted to Protestant Christianity, being influenced by watching George Otis, Jr.'s videos series entitled "Transformation." Those videos also stirred his heart for revival. In 2002, he graduated from Vizayan Nazarene Bible College (VNBC) in Cebu City, earning a Bachelor of Arts degree in Theology with a major in Pastoral Ministry.

Betiwan's Ministerial Background

Church of the Nazarene. From 2002-2009, Betiwan was a minister in the Church of the Nazarene denomination. His first work was pioneering church in Danao, Cebu City. After graduating from VNBC, he served for one year on a 'Jesus Film' Ministry Team, an auxiliary evangelistic arm of the Church of the Nazarene in North Mindanao. In 2003, he was chosen as the lead pastor of the Nazarene church in Iligan City, which he and wife, Myra, served for three years. For undisclosed reasons, he resigned from pastoral leadership there and moved to Dapitan City, Zamboanga del Norte, where they pioneered a ministry under the covering of the Nazarene Evangelistic Team (NET) Missions Group. In 2009, the family returned to Iligan City, where Betiwan became involved in a "body ministry," an intercession ministry for revival in the Philippines and leading a small group of Christians.

NET Missions Fellowship Church, Iligan City. In 2010, Betiwan pioneered a church independent of the Church of the Nazarene called NET Missions Fellowship Church (simply called NET in this study). Unlike the Nazarene denomination with its non-Pentecostal background, NET is a Third-Wave congregation that's open to charismatic manifestations, prophecy, Spirit baptism and speaking in tongues.

Office of the Moral Recovery Program (MRP), Iligan City. In 2013, Betiwan was appointed by the Iligan City mayor as overall-in-charge of the Office of the Moral Recovery Program. This provided a good opportunity for him to minister in the local government, barangay, and schools through preaching and teaching. He still holds the said position and is assisted by seventeen facilitators, most of whom are pastors.

Betiwan's Personal Experience of Revival

Betiwan's knowledge of revival began back in the late 1990s when George Otis Jr.'s "Transformation" videos became popular. His personal experience of a revival, however, occurred in Cebu while still attending Maranatha Christian Fellowship (MCF), an independent Neo-Charismatic church that envisions itself as "a center for revival in Southeast Asia."[77] In one of the revival meetings, he testifies to having experienced "the Glory Presence of God."[78] He writes the following:

> There was deep worship, the atmosphere was ecstatic, people would fall on the ground sometimes by the masses. There was gold dust falling out of nowhere, and people claiming to have gold fillings on their tooth. Weird manifestations like people jerking and vomiting. I remember one conference the room was filled with fog from our waist up, but when we bend down it was very clear. Most of all, my life was changed attending those meetings which became my pursuit—the Glory presence of God.[79]

---

[77] Maranatha Christian Fellowship, "In Revival," Mission/Vision, http://www.maranatha.org.ph/missionvision (accessed July 3, 2019).
[78] Ronald De Asis Betiwan, interview by author, May 26, 2019, transcript, Asia Pacific Research Center, Baguio City, Philippines.
[79] Ibid.

That experience of these manifestations became an important turning point for him in his understanding of revival.

In 2007, during ten days of prayer and fasting, the Lord led him to Isaiah 43:18-19, which stirred his heart to pray for revival in the Philippines. By 2010, he began sharing his understanding of and desire for revival with the young leaders of NET. Due to their lack of experience and understanding of the concept, they didn't respond initially to his exhortation to pray for revival. It was only after the congregation experienced what Betiwan calls "the tangible presence of the Lord" during a church service that most of the NET members involved themselves in intercession for revival, including a two-month around-the-clock prayer ministry.[80]

Interestingly, Betiwan himself received further confirmation of the call to pray for revival when he experienced Spirit baptism during a meeting. He shares: "I was baptized by His tangible presence during our Core [sic] leaders gathering and meeting. From that moment, I started to join with other churches that pray regularly for the tangible presence of the Lord to move in the city and beyond."[81]

Betiwan's Theology of Revival and Signs and Wonders

Revival. Betiwan believes that revival is an experience of the transforming work of God, whereby He turns people from wickedness to righteousness and that it involves a release of divine empowerment. He writes: "It [revival] is also the time of releasing the power of the Spirit of God to His people so that they will be able to do fearlessly and powerfully the command of God."[82]

Betiwan admits that his views on revival were influenced by reading books and hearing revival stories from John and Charles Wesley, from William Seymour of the Azusa Street Revival, and from the Argentinian Revival. He also heard and read about the revivals that occurred in Scotland, China, Indonesia, and other countries. All these stories

---

[80]Ibid.
[81]Ibid.
[82]Ibid.

encouraged Betiwan to believe for revival to happen in the Philippines. He uses Hebrews 13:8 and Acts 2 as bases for his belief in the continuation of the work of God in spiritually reviving nations. It's safe to assume that, for him, revival isn't a transforming and empowering experience just for an individual, but also for a nation.

Signs and Wonders. Betiwan defines signs and wonders as "acts of God manifesting in the lives of the people"[83] and hold that God uses people as vessels in these manifestations. He bases his belief in signs and wonders on Mark 16:17-18, John 14:12, John 17:20, and Hebrews 13:8. While he agrees that signs and wonders are innumerable, he lists in Table 9 a few examples that he personally believes in.[84]

Table 9. Betiwan's Sample List of Signs and Wonders.

1.	Speaking in tongues (both known and unknown tongues)
2.	Prophecy
3.	Healing
4.	Deliverance
5.	Heavenly visitations
6.	Seeing visions
7.	Created miracles, such as multiplication of food, money, etc.
8.	Declaring a word of knowledge
9.	Raising the dead

Betiwan affirms, "I personally experience [sic] these following signs and wonders: deliverance from deep demonic possession and oppression, speak [sic] in other tongues, healing of cancer patients, declaring a word of knowledge and seeing visions." Obviously, for him, these manifestations are present-day realities. In relation to revival, he explains that signs and wonders are primarily used to win souls for Jesus, saying, "The power of God is released to perform wonders and signs so that everyone will believe in the Lord Jesus Christ."[85]

Impartation and Activation. Impartation and activation are terms often used by Neo-Charismatic revivalists when referring to the transfer

---

[83]Ronald De Asis Betiwan, interview by author, May 26, 2019, transcript, Asia Pacific Research Center, Baguio City, Philippines.
[84]Ibid.
[85]Ibid.

and quickening of spiritual gifts in a believer. Regarding *impartation*, Betiwan believes in a "spiritual gifting impartation" (i.e., when one lays hands on, prophesies over, or prays for someone to receive a spiritual gift.[86] He uses 1 Timothy 4:14 and John 20:22 as examples of impartation—the former being when Timothy received a spiritual gift because of the preaching of the word, and the latter when the disciples received a spiritual gift when Jesus breathed on them.[87] Simply said, Betiwan believes that Christians can receive spiritual gifts from other Christians through impartation. Regarding *activation*, Betiwan defines it as "a process of quickening spiritual gifts that have imparted [sic] but never activated because of doubt, lack of knowledge, and other reasons."[88] It is a work of God's Spirit making active a spiritual gift already imparted in a believer for the purpose of accomplishing God's plans.

Betiwan holds that both impartation and activation are acts performed in ministries involved in revival and in signs and wonders and believes that, in revival settings, God uses people as instruments to impart or activate spiritual gifts. However, he does remind that, although impartation and activation are indeed dimensions of the 'greater work' of revival, the more important dimension is prayer and intimacy with God.

Discerning Signs and Wonders. Betiwan admits that, in revival services, some deceptive and erroneous manifestations may occur. In order to avoid such from occurring, he suggests that believers be knowledgeable of the truth. In Table 10, he enumerates the six keys to discerning the validity of signs and wonders.[89]

---

[86]Ibid.
[87]Ibid.
[88]Ronald De Asis Betiwan, interview by author, May 26, 2019, transcript, Asia Pacific Research Center, Baguio City, Philippines.
[89]Ibid.

Table 10. Betiwan's Keys to Discerning Signs and Wonders.

1.	The Word of God. (It must be the foundation and basis of identifying the authentic manifestation of supernatural.
2.	Living a life of righteousness and holiness (Hebrews 12:14).
3.	Intimacy with God, the Source of the supernatural.
4.	Living a life of humility (James 4:6).
5.	Walking and living a life of love and compassion.
6.	Knowledge of how the Enemy works (Ephesians 6:10-18).

Betiwan believes that knowing God's word, living a life of holiness and humility, and maintaining intimacy with God will help in discerning whether a manifestation is from God or not.

Revivalism in the Philippines

Lastly, Betiwan identifies other ministries in the Philippines that operate in the same stream of revivalism. Among them are: Intercessors For the Philippines (IFP) led by Bishop Dan Balais; Hiram Pangilinan and his ministry; Jerome Ocampo and his prayer movement Jesus Revolution Now, and Wayden King's NFS Foundation, which promotes a baptism of love for wounded families.[90]

Summary

In this chapter, the interview data of four Filipino revivalist ministers were presented. All four ministers believe in and demonstrate a revivalist spirituality akin to TB revivalism. They also teach about revival epi-phenomena which they call signs and wonders or glory manifestations.

---

[90] Ibid.

Chapter 8

Understanding the Findings

Analysis and Synthesis of Interview Data

Historical Development of Toronto Blessing Revivalism
in the Philippines

Based on the findings presented above, Toronto-Blessing Revivalism began in the Philippines in the first decade of the millennium. In 2001, Hiram Pangilinan and other Filipino ministers participated in a conference in Pasadena, California, organized by revivalists like Che Ahn.[1] That same year, Pangilinan applied for membership in Ahn's Harvest International Ministries (HIM).[2] By 2005, unusual signs and wonders (otherwise known as glory manifestations) started to appear in the testimonies of Miguel Que.[3]

International TB revivalists also began mentoring Filipino ministers. Here are a few of the more prominent examples:

- 2006— Apollo "Paul" Yadao and wife Ahlmira connected with Leif Hetland in Randy Clark's School of Healing in Lakeville, Minnesota.[4] Hetland became the couple's spiritual father and their church (Destiny Ministries International

---

[1] Hiram Pangilinan, interview by author, February 27, 2018.
[2] Ibid.
[3] Miguel Que, interview by author, December 30, 2018, transcript, Asia Pacific Research Center, Baguio City, Philippines.
[4] Apollo "Paul" Yadao, interview by author, January 20, 2019, transcript, Asia Pacific Research Center, Baguio City, Philippines.

[DMI]) was adopted into Hetland's Global Mission Awareness (GMA).[5]
- 2006—Che Ahn came to the Philippines to conduct a series of revival and transformation meetings.[6]
- 2007—Filipino ministers participated in the Revival Alliance Conference in the United States.[7]
- 2008—Heidi Baker conducted a revival conference in Manila and ministered in Pangilinan's church.[8] Gold dust was said to have been manifested during her ministry.

Hence, the Philippines began to receive the ministry of revivalists who were connected to the TB during that first decade. Some of the reasons for the spread of this spirituality were: the effective use of books, modern media (e.g., the internet, television, videos), itinerant ministries of revivalists, revival conferences locally and abroad, and establishment of revivalist networks connected to mother organizations in North America (e.g., Revival Alliance).

Definition of Signs and Wonders

A conventional content analysis using codes derived from the research points to a basic definition of signs and wonders from the perspective of the four Filipino TB revivalists interviewed. Table 11 shows the result.

---

[5]Ibid.
[6]Hiram Pangilinan, interview by author, February 27, 2018.
[7]Ibid.
[8]Ibid.

Table 11. The Four Filipino TB Revivalists' Conceptual Definition of Signs and Wonders

Question: What is the definition of signs and wonders for Filipino TB Revivalists?			
PARTICIPANT	RESPONSE(S)	INITIAL CODING *(first impression phrases)*	FOCUSED CODING *(categorizing based on conceptual similarity)*
Hiram Pangilinan (Pastor, Church So Blessed International)	"When God comes in His glory, following His glory is a trail of supernatural manifesttations. He opens us up to the things of heaven."[9] "Signs are miracles that point people to Jesus, while wonders are the natural products of the supernatural world invading our world."[10]	In His glory Trail of supernatural manifestations Things of heaven Miracles Natural products of the supernatural world	Supernatural products/ manifestations of heaven and God's glory.
Apollo "Paul" Yadao (Pastor, Destiny Ministries International)	"Miraculous acts of God that demonstrate His power and the supremacy of His	Miraculous acts of God Demonstrate power	Powerful supernatural demonstrations of God and His kingdom.

---

[9] Pangilinan, *Presence Driven*, 220.
[10] Hiram Pangilinan, interview by author, February 27, 2018.

	Kingdom addressing the needs of men through supernatural means and are humanly impossible."[11]	Supremacy of His kingdom Supernatural Humanly impossible	
Miguel Que (Founder, Freshwind Global Ministry and Impact Supernatural School)	"Extraordinary mira-cles that point to Jesus."	Extraordinary miracles Point to Jesus	Miracles with a sign value.
Ronaldo De Asis Betiwan (Pastor, NET Fellow-ship Mission Church)	"Acts of God mani-festing in the lives of the people."[12]	Acts of God Manifesting	Manifestations of God

Based on the code analysis above, these four Filipino TB revivalists define 'signs and wonders' as powerful, supernatural, and divine manifestations with a sign-value, which demonstrates God's glory, kingdom, and heaven. The term 'sign-value' here refers to their perceived value of the other-worldly manifestations as a sign that points to Jesus. However, their perception on how it can serve as a sign to Jesus cannot be derived from the data.

---

[11] Apollo "Paul" Yadao, interview by author, January 20, 2019, transcript, Asia Pacific Research Center, Baguio City, Philippines.

[12] Ronald De Asis Betiwan, interview by author, May 26, 2019, transcript, Asia Pacific Research Center, Baguio City, Philippines.

Interrelating Themes

Apart from their definition of signs and wonders, an analysis of the entire research finding also reveals the following interrelating themes— (1) Manifest Presence of God, (2) Infinite Creativity of God, (3) Literal/Materialized Heaven, (4) Reified Divine Power, and (5) Divine Love. Table 12 shows how these interrelated themes emerge from the research findings.

Table 12. Table of Interrelating Themes.

INTERRELA-TING THEME	DATA SUPPORTING THE THEME	RESEARCH PARTICIPANT	RESEARCHER'S INTERPRETIVE SUMMARY
Manifest Presence of God	Signs and wonders are byproducts of God's manifestation in glory and power.[13] In God's presence, signs and wonders happen.[14]	Hiram Pangilinan	These revivalists claim and propagate that God materializes (manifests) His presence. Signs and wonders in this concept are materializations of God's presence. This repetitive idea of the manifest presence of
	Signs and wonders are supernatural manifestations that show up when God's glory comes in a revival meeting. When God's glory manifests, supernatural manifestations occur.[15]	Apollo "Paul" Yadao	
	Revival happens when God's manifest presence saturates a group of people.[16]	Miguel Que	
	"There was deep worship, the atmosphere was ecstatic, [sic] people would fall on the ground	Ronald De Asis Betiwan	

---

[13] Pangilinan, *Presence Driven,* 227-228.
[14] Ibid., 237.
[15] Apollo "Paul" Yadao, interview by author, January 20, 2019, transcript, Asia Pacific Research Center, Baguio City, Philippines.
[16] Miguel Que, interview by author, December 30, 2018, transcript, Asia Pacific Research Center, Baguio City, Philippines.

	sometimes by the masses. There was gold dust falling out of nowhere, and people claiming to have gold fillings on their tooth. . . . I remember one conference room was filled with fog from our waist up, but when we bend down it was very clear. Most of all my life was changed attending those meetings which became my pursuit—the glory presence of God."[17] The church experienced "tangible presence of the Lord. . . ."[18]		God during revival services sounds a lot like the Latter Rain Movement's theology of the manifest presence, later picked up by John Wimber.
Infinite Creativity of God	God cannot be put in a box; therefore, there are unlimited possibilities of signs and wonders.[19] Signs and wonders can be anything, as long as it is for God's glory.[20]	Hiram Pangilinan	For most of these revivalists, there is no limit to what God can do. Signs and wonders can be anything as long as it's for God's glory. The danger to this mindset, however, is the fallacy of
	When God's glory becomes real and tangible in an assembly, any supernatural manifestation can show up.	Apollo "Paul" Yadao	
	There is no limit to what God can do, and so signs and wonders can be anything.[21]	Miguel Que	

---

[17] Ronald De Asis Betiwan, interview by author, May 26, 2019, transcript, Asia Pacific Research Center, Baguio City, Philippines.

[18] Ibid.

[19] Pangilinan, *Presence Driven*, 232, 237.

[20] Ibid., 237.

[21] Miguel Que, interview by author, December 30, 2018, transcript, Asia Pacific Research Center, Baguio City, Philippines.

			assuming that every supernatural manifestation comes from God.
Literal/ Materialized Heaven	The earthly manifestations of gold dust, gemstones, orbs, angel feathers, and fire are some of the "literal" treasures believers can encounter in heaven.[22] "In an atmosphere of revival…the things of heaven can actually manifest on earth."[23]	Hiram Pangilinan	Most of these revivalists espouse a doctrine of a literal or material heaven. They construct and promote that heaven is composed of earthly elements like gold, gemstones, oil, feathers, clouds, etc. Bible verses that describe heaven like Revelation 21 are seen not figuratively but in a literal and materialistic manner.
	Signs and wonders (e.g., angel feathers, gold dust, gemstone, etc.) demonstrate how God's world is more superior to the material world.[24]	Apollo "Paul" Yadao	
	Signs of Heaven—gemstones (Exodus 39:10-14), feathers (Psalm 91:4), gold dust (Psalm 68:13), the supernatural in pictures, oil (Psalm 23:5), cloud of glory (1 Kings 8:11).	Miguel Que	

---

[22]Pangilinan, *Presence Driven*, 227-228.

[23]Pangilinan, *What if God Comes*, 200.

[24]Apollo "Paul" Yadao, interview by author, January 20, 2019, transcript, Asia Pacific Research Center, Baguio City, Philippines.

Reified Divine Power	When believers love God, He reciprocates by showing us 'heavenly treasures,' that is, glory manifestations.[25]	Hiram Pangilinan	At the heart of their theology is a belief that God purposely reifies his power. For them, God demonstrates or exemplifies what He can do by showing glory manifestations or miraculous acts. They believe that these divine manifestations serve to realize or concretize God's presence, power, and reality in this world.
	"Signs and wonders are miraculous acts of God that demonstrate his power and the supremacy of his kingdom..."[26]	Apollo "Paul" Yadao	
	Power is the evidence of Spirit-baptism.[27]	Miguel Que	
	Signs and wonders are "acts of God mani-festing in the lives of people..."[28] "The power of God is released to perform signs and wonders so that everyone will believe in the Lord Jesus Christ."[29]	Ronald De Asis Betiwan	
Divine Love	"When believers love God, he recipro-cates by showing us 'heavenly treasures,' that is, glory manifestations."[30]	Hiram Pangilinan	Manifestation of signs and wonders for most of

---

[25] Pangilinan, *Presence Driven*, 228.

[26] Apollo "Paul" Yadao, interview by author, January 20, 2019, transcript, Asia Pacific Research Center, Baguio City, Philippines.

[27] Miguel Que, interview by author, December 30, 2018, transcript, Asia Pacific Research Center, Baguio City, Philippines.

[28] Ronald De Asis Betiwan, interview by author, May 26, 2019, transcript, Asia Pacific Research Center, Baguio City, Philippines.

[29] Ibid., 4.

[30] Pangilinan, *Presence Driven*, 228.

	Revival is a divine romance between the Father and his children, sometimes accompanied by epi-phenomena like gold dust, gemstones, gold teeth, etc.	Apollo "Paul" Yadao	them is a manifestation of God's love. It's considered a love token, or a love exchange. If believers "loves on" God, they can receive his love tokens. These love tokens serve to strengthen their intimacy with God.
	Sample signs and wonders God uses to show His love are called 'love tokens.' These include: instant weight change, instant height increase, and instant hair growth.	Miguel Que	
	Maintaining intimacy with God is impor-tant for discerning signs and wonders.	Ronald De Asis Betiwan	

The interrelating themes that emerge from this analysis point to one recurring concept— 'manifestation'. For Filipino TB revivalists, God can manifest His presence, glory, infinite creativity, power, and His literal/materialistic heaven. To manifest in this context is to reify something abstract into something concrete, tangible, or experiential. Thus, for Filipino TB revivalists, the manifestation of signs and wonders (whether biblical or sub-biblical) is the materialization of the divine in a worship (revival) setting.

Conceptual Comparisons

Drawing out the conceptual definition and interrelated themes of TB Revivalism's signs and wonders theology in the Filipino context now allow for a critical evaluation. First, a conceptual comparison between North American TB Revivalism and Filipino TB Revivalism is conducted, then a conceptual comparison is made between Filipino TB revivalist spirituality and Filipino indigenous spirituality.

North American and Filipino Toronto Blessing Revivalist Themes

Earlier in the study, it was hypothesized that Filipino TB Revivalism's signs and wonders theology is similar to that of North American TB Revivalism. In fact, the review of literature showed a direct connection between North American influence and Filipino Revivalism in the P/C tradition. To test that hypothesis, a comparative analysis between North American TB revivalist theology and that of Filipino TB revivalists and made and presented in Table 13.

Table 13. Comparison Between North American and Filipino TB Revivalist Themes.

INTERRELATING THEMES ON SIGNS AND WONDERS	NORTH AMERICAN TB REVIVALISM'S SIGNS AND WONDERS THEOLOGY	FILIPINO TB REVIVALISM'S SIGNS AND WONDERS THEOLOGY	CONCEPTUAL SIMILARITY
Manifest Presence	This is emphasized and magnified especially through repetitive use of the phrase: "encountering the manifest presence of God." Revivalists like Bill Johnson define revival as the manifest presence of God wherein signs and	Signs and wonders are manifested when God is present. Pangilinan, for instance, define signs and wonders as the trail of God's glorious presence.[32] Betiwan, on the other hand, calls it the "glory	Similar

---

[32]Pangilinan, *Presence Driven*, 220.

	wonders continually flow.³¹	presence of God."³³	
Infinite Creativity of God	All agree that there are infinite ways in which God can manifest signs and wonders.	All four agree that God cannot be put in a box, and thus signs and wonders can be anything.	Similar
Literal/Materialized Heaven	The promotion of a literal or material heaven is obvious with their identification of gold dust as coming from streets of heaven, or gemstones in heaven, angels having actual feathers, and so on.	Examples of glory manifestation come from the idea that heaven's streets are gold, gemstones in Revelation 21 are real and tangible, and that angels' have feathers. Que even categorizes a group of signs and wonders as "signs of heaven."³⁴	Similar
Reified Divine Power	They emphasize anointing or divine power as being transferable, as well as manifestation of signs and wonders	All four agree that anointing or power for signs and wonders is transferable via impartation	Similar

---

³¹Bill Johnson, *The Supernatural Power*, 34-35.

³³Ronald De Asis Betiwan, interview by author, May 26, 2019, transcript, Asia Pacific Research Center, Baguio City, Philippines.

³⁴Miguel Que, interview by author, December 30, 2018, transcript, Asia Pacific Research Center, Baguio City, Philippines.

	as proofs of God's power.	and activation. Epi-phenomena are seen as proofs of God's power.	
Divine Love	John Arnott of the Toronto Blessing, together with Clark, Hetland, and other like-minded revivalist, promote a romantic view of God. Manifestation of signs and wonders (e.g., gold dust, gold teeth, gemstones, etc.) are God's means for showing His Fatherly love. For them, it promotes deeper intimacy with God.	Yadao believes in the concept the father's love manifested through signs and wonders. Que identifies a group of signs and wonders as "love tokens." Pangilinan considers it a love exchange.	Similar, although not as equally emphasized by all.

Table 13 reveals a clear similarity between North American TB Revivalism themes and those of Filipino TB Revivalism. The differences lie on the *degree* of emphasis. Some revivalists emphasize the Father's love more, while others emphasize the glory presence of God more. Nevertheless, all five of these interrelated themes emerge from both North American and Filipino TB Revivalisms' signs and wonders theology.

Filipino Indigenous Spirituality Vs. Filipino Toronto Blessing Revivalist Spirituality

Another issue this study tries to highlight is the similarity between TB revivalist spirituality and Filipino indigenous spirituality. The danger of slipping back into an animistic spirituality had been pointed out. To check this concern, a comparison of the interrelating themes between the two spiritualities is made and presented in Table 14. The data used here for Filipino indigenous spirituality are condensed from the review of related literature in Chapter 2.

Table 14. Thematic Similarities Between Filipino Indigenous and TB Revivalist Spirituality.

Interrelating Themes on Signs and Wonders	Filipino TB Revivalist Spirituality	Filipino Indigenous Spirituality	Thematic Similarity
Manifest Presence	God's presence can be manifested or experienced through tangible/experiential phenomena.	The spirits can manifest themselves or their power through different types of phenomena.	Similar
Literal/Materialized Heaven	The things of heaven can manifest on earth.	Concept of heaven is unclear.	Dissimilar
Infinite Creativity of God	God cannot be put in a box. He can manifest His presence and power in infinite ways.	The spirits cannot be limited. They can manifest in different forms and in different ways.	Similar
Reified Divine Power	God's power can be felt or made tangible through His manifestations and can also be transferred	Divine power can be concretely experienced through somatic and phenomenal manifestations.	Similar

	through impartation.	A power acquisition syndrome is observable. Power from deities can be acquired by their followers through rituals and prayers.	
Divine Love	Manifestation of signs and wonders are God's love tokens.	There is no concept of divine love.	Dissimilar

The results of the comparison in Table 14 reveal that three out of the five interrelated themes are shared by both Filipino TB revivalists and the indigenous Filipinos (animists). The animists' view of the divine includes an acceptance of divine manifestation, power reification, and infinite divine creativity.

Thematic Similarities. There are three concepts that are shared by both the Filipino TB revivalists and the Filipino animists. First, both believe that the divine can manifest themselves in various ways; any supernatural phenomena can be a manifestation of divine presence and power. Second, both believe that power exchange is a reality and can be acquired from the divine through prayer and rituals; somatic manifestations and other epi-phenomena (e.g., seeing gold dust, visions, dreams, trances) are considered demonstrations of the supernatural affecting the natural. Third, both believe that the ways and means for divine power to manifest is limitless, there being no constraint as to what the divine can do.

Interpretation of The Findings

Toronto Blessing Revivalism's Signs and Wonders Theology
in the Filipino Perspective

Description

According to the data, manifestations of signs and wonders for Filipino TB revivalists are the reification of both the reality of God and His literal heaven in a revival setting where praise and worship abound. There is both a materialistic and a subjective component to this concept—materialistic in that, for these revivalists, heaven is a material heaven with actual gold, gemstones, angel feathers, etc.; and it is subjective in that it is experience-driven. The experience of the divine can be physical or can occur in an altered state of consciousness (e.g., dreams, visions, trances). For the Filipino TB revivalist, these manifestations are unlimited in kind and style because of the infinite creativity of God.

Also, there is a two-fold purpose for these powerful, supernatural, and miraculous manifestations. First, they serve as a sign that points to the reality of a supernatural God; and second, they serve to deepen relationship through heightened awareness of the divine and through experiential (albeit subjective) proofs of God's reality. Thus, for Filipino TB revivalists, manifestations of signs and wonders are indicative reifications of the divine, which occur in revivalism contexts.

Antecedents

The data also reveal that Filipino TB revivalist' signs and wonders theology is similar to that of North American TB revivalists. In fact, as the analysis above demonstrates, the former's signs and wonders theology has thematic similarities to the latter. For instance, the most common theme among their theologies is represented by the parlance, "manifest presence." Both North American and Filipino TB revivalists agree that signs and wonders are manifestations of God's presence, glory, and power. For them, these manifestations (whether biblical or sub-biblical) are normative outcomes of divine reification.

Filipino TB revivalist theology of signs and wonders also share thematic similarities with Filipino indigenous religion. Both view the manifestation of the divine as realities. In other words, the supernatural or other-worldly can invade the natural or this-worldly aspects of life. Also, they both display a power-acquisition syndrome, where the transfer or acquisition of power meets socio-religious expectations and are best experienced in ritual settings—i.e., praise and worship for TB revivalists, prayer and ritual for animists). Lastly, both also consider supernatural phenomena as diverse and unconstrained, since divine power is limitless.

Chapter 9

Evaluation from a Classical Pentecostal Perspective

The data in Chapter 7 confirms that, indeed, Filipino Toronto-Blessing Revivalism's signs and wonders theology is similar to that of North American TB Revivalism. This narrow stream of revivalist spirituality, which entered the country in the first decade of the millennium, has successfully influenced some Filipino ministers. The four who were interviewed for this study proved to be a rich source of information in understanding their signs and wonders theology as well as their revivalist spirituality.

With these findings, it is now possible to evaluate the implications of their theological claims from a Classical Pentecostal perspective. This chapter provides two critical responses. First is an acknowledgement of the positive implications of this revivalist spirituality to the P/C Movement in the Philippines. Second is an acknowledgment of its precarious implications. The chapter ends with a proposition for the P/C Movement in the Philippines.

The Positive Implications

Amid the controversy over this narrow stream of revivalism in the Philippines, the emergence and continued development of the revivalists' pronounced spirituality has positive implications for the P/C Movement. For one thing, this spirituality meets the Filipino Christian's innate need for deeper psycho-spiritual commitment. In Chapter 5, a socio-religious exegesis of the Philippines reveals that, at the root of Filipino Christianity, is an indigenous worldview which believes in the direct relationship of divine worship/patronage to human circumstance. The line between the supernatural and the natural is blurred (in fact, almost non-existent). Inherent in each Filipino is a belief that the supernatural is directly connected to the natural affairs of people. Thus, rituals and intercession (or in this case, prayer, praise, and worship) becomes means of communication between the supernatural and the natural.

The motivation behind this spirituality is the need to encounter divine power, which Aigbe calls 'a power acquisition syndrome'.[1] Filipinos believe in divine power, want to experience divine power, and are thrilled with tangible proofs of that power. Sensate experiences of the divine not only amaze, but also fill up an indigenous need for psycho-spiritual encounters. Encounters such as these are used as proofs of divine existence and divine participation in people's this-worldly affairs.

Looking back on the superimposition of Spanish Catholicism and American Protestantism in the Filipino religious soil, both traditions were able to satisfy the 'ultimate concerns' of religion, which included God, salvation, sin, and heaven/hell. However, neither were able to develop a spiritual framework for 'this-worldly concerns'. There remained within the Filipino mind questions on the divine's participation and relevance to daily life concerns.[2] Absence of a sufficient framework to meet this religious need resulted in a split-level Christianity (or Folk Catholicism), where Christianity and Filipino indigenous spirituality existed in the same religious plane.[3]

Development of TB Revivalism within the P/C tradition of Christianity in the Philippines gives a possible solution to this problem. TB revivalist spirituality, with its similarities to indigenous spirituality, can provide the spiritual framework for the divine's reality and participation in daily life affairs through their signs and wonders theology.

For Filipino TB revivalists, manifestations of signs and wonders are indicative reifications of the divine, which occur in revivalism contexts. The practice of revivalism, then, becomes a conduit for experiencing divine power; and the experience of sensate and sub-biblical phenomena (sometimes claimed as God's signs and wonders) become indications of the reality and concreteness of that power in a person's this-worldly experience. Thus, through this revivalist spirituality, the Filipino's need

---

[1] Aigbe, 338.
[2] Bulatao, "Split-Level Christianity," 120.
[3] Ibid.

for deeper psycho-spiritual commitment is met with Christian rituals and symbols. It also addresses the chief issue of divine power, which is an inherent dimension in Filipino spirituality. Simply said, a TB revivalist spirituality, with its theology of signs and wonders, can contribute to enhancing Filipino Christian spirituality.[4]

Precarious Implications

That being said, this particular revivalist spirituality also has precarious implications. The existence of a split-level Christianity in the Philippines is double-edged in that it could positively lead to a contextualized Christian spirituality OR it could negatively lead to syncretism—the coalescence of Christianity with folk beliefs and practices.

The danger of slipping into syncretism can be illustrated by Kim Jong Fil's proposed model of a double-structured religious system among churches/movements in the greater Manila area.[5] Although limited to a specific geographical location, this model can be representative of the existing religious system in the Philippines. Table 15 is my adaptation and modification of Kim's model.[6] It includes a list of modern-day religious structures both in the Philippines and in TB revivalism.[7]

---

[4] Jae Yong Jong's study on Filipino Pentecostal Spirituality supports this contention through the concept of "empowered biblical transformation." He posits that Filipino indigenous spirituality can be used by God as a jumping board towards a Spirit-empowered spirituality in the Filipino context. In this sense, TB Revivalism in the Filipino P/C tradition through the framework of 'empowered biblical transformation' may result to a contextualized Filipino Christian spirituality. See Jae, 238-239.
[5] Kim, 144.
[6] A comprehensive discussion of this proposed religious structure can be found in Kim's dissertation. See Kim, 142-168.
[7] Ibid., 144, 313.

Table 15. Double-Structured Religious Systems in the Philippines.

RELIGIOUS LEVEL	PRE-SPANISH ERA	SPANISH ERA	AMERICAN ERA	MODERN ERA
Upper level	No importance of western religion	Hispanized Ro-man Catholicism	Protestantism	Roman Catholicism
				Protestantism
Reciprocal Interaction[8]			Pentecostalism	Charismatics (Catholics)
				Charismatic Catholics Classical Pentecostals
Lower Level		Folk Catholicism		Popular Catholics
				Popular Catholic Charismatics
				Neo-Charismatics /Third Wavers
				TB Revivalism[9]
Animism	Ancient religious beliefs and practices	Retaining Indigenous Religion		Mysticism
				Spiritualists
				Cults

Table 15 displays a split-level religious system in the country. The *upper level* structures are the institutionalized and/or established churches, such as the institutionalized Roman Catholic Church and those within established Protestant denominations. The *reciprocal interaction level*, according to Kim, includes contemporary movements, which have shown integration of the country's three major religious structures—Indigenous Filipino, Catholicism, and Protestantism.[10] Kim proposes

---

[8]Kim explains that churches or movements within the reciprocal interaction level are those that have integrated the three major religions of: Indigenous Filipino, Catholicism, and Protestantism into its religious structure. Kim, 145-146.

[9]I inserted TB revivalism in this table because it is a narrow stream of revivalism within the Neo-Charismatic movement. It also has similarities to animism, especially in their theology of signs and wonders, which place them closer to mysticism.

[10]Kim, "Contemporary Pentecostal Charismatic Movements," 145-146.

that Classical Pentecostalism and Charismatics fit this reciprocal interaction level structure.[11] The *lower level* structures are folk or popular religious movements. Kim positions the Third Wavers in this level because of their views on Charismatic faith healing and deliverance, which, for him, display features of "new mysticism."[12]

In light of this, I added TB Revivalism in the lower level structure just below the Third Wave Movement for these reasons—(1) it is a narrow stream of revivalist spirituality within the Neo-Charismatic/Third Wave circle, (2) it has thematic similarities with animism, and (3) it is identified as a form of Christian mysticism by scholars like Margaret Poloma.[13] Also note that TB Revivalism sits closer to *animism*, its position in a double-structured religious system is just a touch above mysticism. Thus, it hangs in a precarious balance between offering a contextualized Christian religion and offering a folk mystical religion.

This is a danger for Filipino P/C believers, whose deep psycho-spiritual needs and easy acceptance of supernatural phenomena in daily life affairs can result in the coalescence of folk mysticism in their Christian theology and practice, possibly resulting in a kind of folk Pentecostalism, which feeds the need for mystical power encounters more than the need for a redemptive Gospel. Furthermore, its precarious leaning toward folk mysticism also endangers P/C believers to other theological pitfalls.

In their book, *Understanding Folk Religion,* Paul Hiebert, R. Daniel Shaw, and Tite Tiénou identified seven theological pitfalls that can be related to TB Revivalism.[14] Table 16 is a condensed version of their discussion.[15] I added a column of brief explanations as to how these pitfalls are dangerous to TB Revivalism.

---

[11]Ibid.
[12]For a more comprehensive discussion of this, see Kim, 313-336.
[13]Poloma, *Main Street Mystics,* 27-29.
[14]Hiebert, Shaw, and Tiénou, 378-381.
[15]Ibid.

Table 16. Pitfalls of Folk Religion in Relation to TB Revivalism.

PITFALL	EXPLANATION	DANGER TO TB REVIVALISM[16]
1. Syncretism	One theme present in folk religion is that of magical powers. It is an underlying assumption that, when coalesced with elements of Christian teaching, may cause the Gospel to lose its integrity and message.	A spirituality that emphasizes the supernatural excessively may be victim to a magical mentality. Magic may result in god-like assumptions (i.e., humans having supernatural power). If not pastored, magical mentality may supersede biblical mentality in TB revivalism.
2. Human-centeredness	Androcentrism is a result of religions created by humans. In folk religions, people become too self-centered, thinking that everything revolves around them and their lives. Religion becomes an avenue to get what they desire.	Renewal services in TB Revivalism mostly focus on individual catharsis. Believers come to experience God; they come to receive power, healing, miracles, and love tokens (e.g., gemstones, feathers). For them, manifestations of signs and wonders have become sources of pleasure and awe. This self-centeredness could result to human-centeredness.
3. Experience based theology	Folk religion is experience based, with a primary concern for power rather than truth. There is a tendency to accept	TB revivalists accept sub-biblical phenomena on the basis of testimonies. Some revivalists commit the fallacy of

---

[16] I added this column as a way to connect the theological pitfalls suggested by Hiebert, Shaw, and Tiénou to TB revivalist spirituality.

	testimonies or reports without proper verification. Phenomenological claims are often confused as ontological realities, even without sufficient bases. For example, in folk religion there are many testimonies and reports of visions, trances, miracles, guidance through divination, etc.	attributing all types of phenomena as God's work. Yet, not all phenomena come from God. Some can be false signs or are simply carnal/fleshly demonstrations. The tendency to proof text the Bible so as to support sub-biblical experiences aggravates this problem. A theology that normatively promotes sub-biblical experiences on the basis of proof-texted verses and/or testimony alone is walking on a slippery slope.
4. Reinforcing secularism	The authors explained the connection of secularism to folk religion in this manner—"By looking for supernatural events as manifestations of God's presence, they imply that God is not directly at work in natural phenomena that are studied by science. But as the knowledge of science grows, God is increasingly pushed to the margins of life. Moreover, as miracles become routine, they no longer appear extraordinary, and people look for new and more spectacular miracles to reassure themselves that God is with them. The net	The corollary effect of overemphasizing signs and wonders as proofs of the "manifest presence or power of God" is the mistaken belief that He is not present in the natural. The dichotomy between the natural and supernatural may result in the unwanted effect of one's unawareness of God's presence in the ordinary or mundane activities of life. This contributes to a secular mind-set, where the worship of God is removed from the daily normal activities of living.

	effect of these dynamics is the secularization of everyday life."[17]	
5. Generating false guilt	Folk religion often promotes and rejoices over the extraordinary ways of God but is not able to deal with non-healing or injustice.	Overemphasis on miracles and signs and wonders also results in neglect of those who are suffering non-healing, failure, and injustice. Those who go through these downfalls may feel guilty that they are not part of the victories of God. This is a false and destructive guilt.
6. Imbalance	In folk religion, there is a misplaced 'center of spirituality', with Christ ushered to the periphery. At the center of a folk spirituality can be peace, healing, justice, or deliverance. Christ justifies their concerns, but His person, message, and mission does not necessarily become their center.	TB revivalists have different emphases. Some put emphasis on *shalom* (peace) and spiritual healing, some on supernatural kingdom advancement, some on deliverance and spiritual warfare, some on miraculous kingdom living, some on divine intimacy. On their own, these are not wrong themes, but they do not represent the entirety of Jesus' message and mission.
7. Exalting the leader	Folk religions usually have leaders who are charismatic, authoritarian, and prophetic. Followers of these religions may	Although TB Revivalism is ideally a lay empowering movement; in reality, all TB revivalist ministries are known

---

[17]Hiebert, Shaw, and Tiénou, *Understanding Folk Religion*, 380.

	end up exalting their leaders because of their giftedness.	for their charismatic leaders. For example: John Arnott is known for CTF, Randy Clark for ANGA, Bill Johnson for Bethel, Che Ahn for HIM, Heidi Baker for IRIS, etc. In the Philippines, Hiram Pangilinan is more famous than his church, CSBI. These leaders are spiritually-gifted, can move in signs and wonders, and thus can gather a following. Although the leaders mentioned here appear humble and down-to-earth in person, their charismatic appeal still poses a risk for exaltation.

The discussion above demonstrates that TB Revivalism and its signs and wonders theology has precarious implications. Aside from a potential danger of syncretism, there is also the danger of reinforcing secularism, theological imbalance, human-centeredness, magical mentality, and the like. Indeed, these implications only point to the need for a balanced theology of signs and wonders in this revivalist movement. Perhaps Hiebert, Shaw, and Tiénou were correct when they wrote, "the Church must avoid making miracles the signs of God's presence, and the center of its attention and ministry."[18] As the findings above show, an overemphasis on the supernatural may displace the centrality of Christ in the life and ministry of the church.

---

[18]Ibid.

A Way Forward

The Need for Biblical Discernment

Recognizing both the positive and the dangerous implications of this revivalist spirituality leads us now to understand the precarious dilemma that the Filipino P/C Movement is in. One cannot shrug off the importance of a revivalist spirituality in a country with an inherent need for deep psycho-spiritual encounters. And while one should not decry genuine revival in the P/C tradition simply because of theological dangers, neither can one ignore the dangers of a revivalist spirituality superimposed on an inherently animistic worldview like that of Filipino Christians. Perhaps the way forward is to establish a framework of discernment for manifestations of signs and wonders.

This is especially necessary for TB Revivalism, since the main problem is its uncritical acceptance of epi-phenomena as normative. Such uncritical acceptance is risky because not all supernatural manifestations come from God. In fact, they are reported in other non-Christian religions or mystical movements.[19] The Bible, too, warns of the existence of false signs and wonders (Exodus 7:11; Matthew 24:24; Thessalonians 2:9; Revelation 13:13-14, 16:14, 19:20) and admonishes believers to test the spirits (1 Corinthians 12:3, 1 Thessalonians 5:20-21, 1 John 4:1-6). Thus, it makes sense to critically examine supernatural phenomena through the lens of biblical discernment.

Hiebert, Shaw, and Tiénou rhetorically discuss how biblical discernment in dealing with folk religion can be observed and assert that the Bible provides at least the following eight tests of confirming God's work:

> Does it give the glory to God rather than to humans (John 8:50, 12:27-28, 17:4, 17:18)? Around the world today people are drawn to strong personalities and tend to deify them. This is particularly true in folk religions. Does it recognize the lordship of Christ (James 2:14-19; 1 John 2:3-5, 5:3)? The test here is not one of orthodoxy but of submission to Christ in humility and obedience. Is the evidence of God's power through the

---

[19]For examples read, Hiebert, Shaw, Tiénou, *Understanding Folk Religion,* 375.

Holy Spirit emphasized or manifestations of the flesh? Does it conform to scriptural teaching? Are those involved willing to submit their lives and teachings to the test of Scripture? Are the leaders and people accountable to others in the church? The interpretation of Scripture is not a personal matter but a concern of the church as a hermeneutical community. Do those involved manifest the fruits of the Spirit (Galatians 5:22-25)? Is there love or self-centeredness, patience or short-temperedness, gentleness or arrogance? Does the teaching and practice lead believers toward spiritual maturity (1 Corinthians 12-14)? Some things are characteristic of spiritual immaturity, which should be left behind as Christians grow spiritually. Does it lead Christians to seek the unity of the body of Christ or is it divisive (John 17:11; 1 John 2:9-11, 5:1-2)? This does not mean that divisions will not occur but that the teachings lead believers to a sense of spiritual superiority or have led them astray.[20]

These questions are presented for the purpose of honest evaluation. Since revivalism is a mixed brew of the divine and the flesh, it is only right for its participants to willingly measure every experience through the yardstick of the Bible. Thus, the idea of biblical discernment is not to approach supernatural phenomena with upfront skepticism, but rather with openness to and love for the truth of God's word. Any experience that falls short of God's word may be considered an extraordinary experience but not a normative one.

---

[20]Ibid.

Chapter 10

Evaluating Manifestations

Proposal: A Qualitative Scale for Evaluating Manifestations

Perhaps a way to objectively evaluate manifestations claimed as signs and wonders is through the use of a qualitative rating scale. This scale would ideally measure the biblical rootedness of a manifestation by answering these four close-ended questions—(1) Does the manifestation have biblical precedent? (2) Can the manifestation be used to point to the salvific purposes of God? (3) Does the manifestation glorify God, not humans or other beings? (4) Does the manifestation conform to scriptural teaching?

Q.1—Does a Manifestation Have Biblical Precedent?

Biblical precedent here refers to biblical examples of signs and wonders that can serve as a model for signs and wonders today. Examples of such manifestations with biblical precedents are categorically summarized by Norman Geisler as power over non-human nature (Matthew 8:26, 14:14-21, 14:24-33; Mark 6:34-44, 8:1-9; Luke 5:1-11; John 2:1-11), power to raise the dead (Luke 7:11-15, John 11:17-44), and power over all kinds of diseases (Matthew 8:2-4; Mark 6:8, 8:22-26; Luke 5:12-16; John 5:1-9).[1] Geisler posits that in the Bible these three categories demonstrate the extent of God's miracles and signs and wonders.[2]

---

[1] Norman Geisler, *Signs and Wonders,* (Wheaton, IL: Tyndale House Publishers, Inc., 1988), 25, 147-148.
[2] Ibid.

Since animistic religions (including those in the Philippines) do have varieties of signs and wonders that resemble those in TB Revivalism, biblical precedents can provide safeguards for Filipino Pentecostal believers whose inherent supernatural worldview predisposes them into folk spirituality.[3] Geisler warns, "Every mystery is not a miracle. Not everything supernormal is supernatural. There are many things that are odd; but all are not of God."[4] Therefore, one must have a yardstick for determining which is of God and which is not. Since Scripture clearly instructs believers to differentiate truth and error by examining the Bible daily (Acts 17:11), assessing manifestations through the criteria of biblical precedents is necessary.

Q.2—Can the Manifestation Be Used to Point to the Salvific Purposes of God?

God never used signs and wonders in a trivial manner; there was always a purpose to His divine activity. For instance, in the Old Testament, they were part and parcel of His salvific purposes. Roger Cotton writes, "The terms for signs and wonders used in the Old Testament refer to supernatural, spectacular acts and events clearly beyond human ability, eliciting awe or amazement in people and pointing to something about God and His saving purpose."[5] Deuteronomy 7:19 best illustrates this when Moses said, *"You saw with your own eyes the great trials, the signs and wonders, the mighty hand and outstretched arm, with which the LORD your God brought you out. The LORD your God will do the same to all the peoples you now fear."* Moses' encouragement demonstrates how God used signs and wonders in those days—not just to prove His supremacy, but also to

---

[3] One proof of this predisposition is Dave Johnson's research amongst the Filipino Waray AGs, which pointed out how few aspects of these Classical Pentecostals' spirituality are still reflective of their animistic past. See Dave Johnson, *Theology in Context*, 165-178.

[4] Geisler, *Signs and Wonders*, 47.

[5] Roger D. Cotton, ""Wonderful—God's Name" in *Signs & Wonders in Ministry Today*, eds. Benny C. Aker and Gary B. McGee (Springfield, MO: Gospel Publishing House, 1996), 22; J. Rodman Williams, *Renewal Theology* (Grand Rapids, MI: Zondervan, 1988), vol. 1, 141-144; Wayne Grudem, "Should Christians Expect Miracles Today?" in *The Kingdom and the Power: Are Healing and the Spiritual Gifts Used by Jesus and the Early Church Meant for the Church Today?*, eds. Gary S. Greig and Kevin N. Springer (Ventura, CA: Regal Books, 1993), 100-102.

deliver His people from slavery. No doubt they amazed people; but more importantly, they opened a pathway for salvation and deliverance. This is true as well in the New Testament. Benny Aker writes,

> 'Signs and wonders' emerge as one of the several categories of miracles in the New Testament. They belong to a special class, describing God's saving activity when people respond by faith to the gospel—they are the necessary events to deliver sinners bound by sin in its various dimensions.[6]

Signs and wonders in the New Testament were always linked with God's salvation-deliverance. In fact, Aker explains that whenever the word 'signs' (Gk. *semeion*) and the word 'wonders' (Gk. *teras*) occur together in the New Testament, it's always in "evangelistic contexts and manifests God's salvation."[7] Hence, these manifestations in the News Testament were never just about amazing people of God's presence and power, they were always purposefully linked to His work of salvation-deliverance. As Aker aptly writes, "Signs and wonders happen in the forefront of evangelism where the gospel of the Kingdom works to free people from sin and its complex, imprisoning effects."[8]

Menzies and Menzies support this position by pointing out that signs and wonders are incidental to the preaching of the Gospel.[9] They argue that, in Luke-Acts, proclamation or verbal witness to the Gospel (not miracle-working power) was the primary result of Spirit-empowerment.[10] Manifestations of signs and wonders, then, can only be truly biblical when they accompany proclamation of the Gospel and are useful for pointing people towards Jesus as Savior. From this, one can conclude that there is no such thing as 'purposeless phenomena' in God's meta-narrative. Signs and wonders are connected to His salvation-deliverance message.

Interestingly, New Testament data reveal that manifestation of signs and wonders were more rampant in evangelistic settings, where there was a

---

[6]Benny C. Aker, "The Gospel in Action," in *Signs and Wonders in Ministry Today*, eds. Benny C. Aker and Gary B. McGee (Springfield, MO: Gospel Publishing House, 1996), 42.
[7]Ibid., 34.
[8]Ibid., 43.
[9] Menzies and Menzies, *Spirit and Power*, 145-156.
[10]Ibid., 149.

need to reveal Jesus as the Savior, than in a believers' community, where people already accepted Jesus. Art Glasser explains it well:

> When we consider the biblical data, we discover that a distinct shift in emphasis exists between the gospel and Acts and the remainder of the New Testament. While gospel presents Jesus as a miracle worker and the Acts portray certain key persons in the early church as performing miracles, Paul in his epistles seems reluctant to recall his own involvement in this activity and even downgrades its importance. Rather, he, James and the apostle John stress ethical concerns and call attention to the need for discernment, for testing the spirits. Their approach to spiritual realities is greatly different from charismatic emphases.[11]

In other words, in the Gospels and in Acts, manifestations of signs and wonders were rampant because of the need to proclaim Jesus as the Christ. Their main purpose was revelation—i.e., serving to draw people's attention and point them to the Savior (John 3:1-21).

However, when reading the epistles, one can see that, whenever Paul, Peter, James, and John talked to the believing community, their emphases were more on social and ethical concerns, growing in holiness and personal character, growing in corporate character, practicing love, fulfilling the eschatological goal of global evangelism, etc. In the latter part of the New Testament, those in the believing community were expected to go beyond a preoccupation with signs and wonders and instead involve themselves in the process of spiritual maturity, both individually and as a community.

This shift in emphases in the New Testament supports the contention that signs and wonders were observed more in evangelistic contexts, where there was a need to reveal Jesus as the Savior and to confirm the Gospel message of the kingdom of God. However, once people entered into the believing community, the emphases shifted to personal and corporate kingdom-living. Thus, biblical data strongly point to the manifestation of signs and wonders as miraculous phenomena that serve

---

[11] Art Glasser, "The Miraculous in Ministry," in *Wonders and the Word: An Examination of Issues Raised by John Wimber and the Vineyard Movement*, ed. James R. Coggins and Paul G. Hiebert (Winnipeg, MB, Canada: Kindred Press, 1989), 100.

as a witness to the salvation-deliverance of God. They are more aptly used in evangelism in order that non-believers may encounter the power of God and then believe.

So, in assessing signs and wonders today, one must determine if the manifestation can be used to point to the salvation-deliverance of the Lord. Is it effective in ushering people into saving faith? If not, then perhaps it is not a biblically rooted manifestation of signs and wonders.

Q.3—Does the Manifestation Glorify God, Not Humans or Other Beings?

Hiebert, Shaw, and Tiénou discussed in their book, *Understanding Folk Religion*, the pitfall of human-centeredness in folk religions.[12] There is a tendency to honor a charismatic person when that person demonstrates extraordinary capacities. Paul Hiebert considers believers in North America at risk of this pitfall because "people tend to follow strong personalities."[13]

This pitfall is also possible in the Philippines. The country's socio-religious background (presented in Chapter 5) reveals a pre-Christian religious system that tends to deify humans who exhibit power or 'other beings' with supernatural capacities. For pre-Christian Filipinos, effectiveness of powers is the bases for allegiance. If humans or other beings demonstrate powers that are effective in meeting felt needs, then the people tend to give allegiance to them.

In light of this, it's important to carefully evaluate if a manifestation of signs and wonders glorifies God and not humans or other beings. Effectiveness in meeting felt needs should not be the criterion for judging signs and wonders; rather, they should be judged as to their effectiveness in directing people's attention to God. If they do not glorify God or lead people to knowing Jesus as Savior and Lord, then they are not truly biblical signs and wonders.

Admittedly, this third qualitative question is difficult to answer because supernatural manifestations are not self-authenticating. However, for signs and wonders to be considered biblical manifestations, they should not redirect allegiance from God to humans or other beings.

---

[12] Hiebert, Shaw, and Tiénou, 378-381.
[13] Paul Hiebert, "Healing and the Kingdom," in *Wonders and the Word*, 136.

If a manifestation has a higher tendency to result in a fanfare of charismatic leaders or beings like angels, other saints, or spirits, then it is glorifying these human actors or other beings, not God.

A manifestation of signs and wonders glorifies God by confirming His nature and His word. God is the God who saves, and the Bible is His meta-narrative of salvation. Hebrews 2:3-4 reminds the believing community that the salvation they received was confirmed first by those who were Jesus' witnesses and second by miracles, signs and wonders. In other words, God did not use signs and wonders as ends in themselves, but rather as means to reveal Himself and to attest to His message. A manifestation that is not congruent with the nature and message of God is not a biblical signs and wonders.

Q.4—Does the Manifestation Conform to Scriptural Teachings?

As mentioned above, congruence to God's nature and His word is essential in evaluating a manifestation. Since the Bible is His written self-revelation, it is the appropriate yardstick for miracles and/or supernatural manifestations. It is also the primary source for all theology and provides the norm against which all doctrines are to be evaluated. Many people immediately think that all supernatural manifestations are of God, but that isn't true. Hiebert points out that signs and wonders should not be associated only with God,[14] saying, "Pharaoh's magicians did signs (Ex. 7:10-22) and so do Satan (2 Thess. 2:9) and false prophets (Matt. 24:24). They are not proofs of God's presence—they themselves need to be tested for their source."[15] Thus, it is wrong to assume that just because something is extraordinary or supernatural it comes from God. If a manifestation does not conform to God's nature, to His salvific work, to the truths He has revealed, and to His moral norms, then one must consider that it is not of God.

---

[14]Hiebert, "Healing and the Kingdom," in *Wonders and the Word*, 131.
[15]Ibid.

Geisler summarizes the difference between true and counterfeit miracles in Table 17.

Table 17. Geisler's Summary of the Differences Between True and Counterfeit Miracles.[16]

TRUE MIRACLES	COUNTERFEIT MIRACLES
Actual supernatural acts	Extraordinary natural acts
Supernatural directed	Naturally directed
Supernatural intervention	Natural operation
Always associated with truth	Always associate with error
Connected with true prophets	Connected with false prophets
Connected with biblical teaching	Connected with unbiblical teaching
Always associated with good	Always associated with evil
Glorify the Creator	Glorify the creature
Promote moral good which benefits God's creation	Promote moral evil which destroys God's creation
Fit with nature	Misfit with nature
Are not unnatural	Are unnatural (odd)

In this summary, a true miracle (or signs and wonders) is associated with truth, congruent with biblical teaching, and associated with the moral good espoused by the Bible. A counterfeit is associated with error, evil, and unbiblical teaching. This informs us that there is a limitation to biblical manifestation of signs and wonders—a limitation defined by God's truth, goodness, and revealed will as written in the Bible. A true manifestation of signs and wonders must then be within the framework of biblical teaching and God's moral standards. Any manifestation that ventures outside of these parameters is considered sub-biblical and non-normative.

In order to see the viability of this proposed framework, the following section will apply a qualitative assessment on one manifestation—gold dust, which has been identified by all TB revivalists as a manifestation of signs and wonders. The four questions posed above

---

[16]Geisler, Signs and Wonders, 125.

will be used to evaluate the accuracy of their claim. A rationale for the rating will be given after the assessment.

Case Study: Assessing the Manifestation of Gold Dust

Filipino TB revivalists claim that gold dust is a normative manifestation of signs and wonders that occurs when God manifests His presence. They hold that gold dust comes from the pavements of heaven and consider this manifestation as God's way of amazing His people as well as affirming a literal heaven with streets of gold. In Table 18, the manifestation of gold dust is assessed according to the answers to the four questions addressed above.

Table 18. Assessment on the Manifestation of Gold Dust.

MANIFESTATION 1: GOLD DUST			
Criteria	Yes	No	Maybe
Q.1—Is there biblical precedent for it?	X	✓	X
Q.2—Is it effective in pointing to the Gospel?	X	✓	X
Q.3—Does it give glory to God, not humans or other beings?	X	✓	X
Q.4—Does it conform to scriptural teaching?	X	✓	X
Tally:	0	4	0

The table shows that out of a possible score of 4, the possibility of gold dust being a biblical manifestation of signs and wonders is zero.

Rationale

Question 1. There is no biblical precedent of gold dust in either the Old Testament or the New. Not once in the Bible was it mentioned that gold dust manifested during evangelistic settings or in the believers' community. In fact, there is no mention at all of gold dust in the Bible.

Question 2. Gold dust does not have any reference point to the Gospel or to Jesus Christ. His miracles never included manifestations of gold or gold dust, nor did His disciples work miracles involving gold.

That being the case, how then can gold dust point to salvation? Perhaps one can argue that the manifestation of gold dust attests to a literal/materialistic heaven with streets of gold. If so, then use that as a point of reference for the need of a savior to enter that heaven. However, such a hypothetical argument has the following three weaknesses.

First—It can only be effective if the occurrence of gold dust is always accompanied by the preaching of the Gospel. However, in most cases, the appearance of gold dust occurs during renewal services where the majority of recipients are already believers. The evangelistic preaching of the Gospel rarely happens in TB revival services, because the focus of these services is a cathartic experience of divine presence.[17]

Second—This manifestation has never been connected to the salvific work of Christ. Instead, it is always connected to the assumed existence of a literal/materialistic heaven. For instance, Pangilinan rationalizes it is proof that heaven is colorful.[18] Que categorizes it as a sign of heaven.[19] Hence, even the TB revivalists usually identify it as a manifestation that points to heaven, rather than a sign and wonder that points to Jesus.

Existence of a literal/materialistic heaven with streets of gold is not accepted by most biblical scholars. The understanding of gold dust from heaven stems from Revelation 21:18 and 21, leading TB revivalists to rationalize that the gold in heaven can manifest on earth through gold dust and gold teeth. However, most biblical scholars argue that this description of the new heaven was contained in apocalyptic language, such that it probably referred to the Jewish expression of "Jerusalem the Golden."[20] David Aune explains that this expression probably came "from the uniform color of the yellow sandstone out of which most of the city was and is constructed."[21]

Pentecostal scholars J. Christopher Thomas and Frank Macchia argue that the vision probably alludes to 1 Kings 6:30, where one can

---

[17]For example, Margaret Poloma, in her study of CTF (the home of the TB phenomena), concluded that the rate of conversion during their services was only 1%. This means that 99% of attendees were already believers. See Poloma, Inspecting the Fruit of the 'Toronto Blessing': A Sociological Perspective," 57-64.

[18]Pangilinan, *Presence Driven,* 220-235.

[19]Miguel Que, messenger interview by author, December 30, 2018, transcript, Asia Pacific Research Center, Baguio City, Philippines.

[20]David E. Aune, "Revelation 17-22," *Word Biblical Commentary* vol. 52C, ed. Bruce Metzger (Waco, TX: Word Books, 1998), 1164.

[21]Ibid.

read how Old Testament priests ministered on a floor inlaid with gold.[22] This allusion also fits the explanation of the precious stones in Revelations 21:21, which functioned to emphasize the priestly status of the people of God in this eschatological Jerusalem.[23] So, with proper historical-grammatical analysis of the text, the idea of literal dust coming down on earth from the pavement of heaven sounds trivial. Instead, the figurative language used was intended to help readers see the deeper sense of the passage—i.e., the eschatological glory and majesty of the New Jerusalem, where God will dwell in the midst of His people.

Clearly then, the concept of gold dust from heaven falling on people today has weak exegetical support. Ultimately, it does not function as an effective sign of the salvation message of Jesus.

Third—Because it magnifies the concept of a literal heaven more than God's nature and salvific purposes, it does not glorify God. He reveals himself in Scripture as an all-wise, all-powerful Father who wants to be in a personal relationship with His people. Frequently, He works in the natural or regularities of people's lives; infrequently, in the supernatural.

As to God's interaction with His people, Cotton writes, "According to scriptural precedent, God's direct, spectacular acts for His people will be carefully chosen and infrequent. More often, God interacts with His creation in unspectacular ways, which should be considered a normal part of life."[24] He normally interacts with His people through natural ways, only intervening supernaturally when He needs to attest to His supremacy and His message of salvation-deliverance. Like a wise parent, God doesn't use supernatural manifestations to spoil His children and continually 'wow' them; rather He uses them with purpose and proper timing.

Question 3. The idea of God manifesting gold dust to amaze people about a golden-paved or colorful heaven is not congruent to His self-revelation in Scripture. While His signs and wonders were spectacular and awe-inspiring, their purpose was to point people to both His supremacy and His offer of salvation. To remove God's supernatural

---

[22] John Christopher Thomas and Frank D. Macchia, *Revelation*. The Two Horizons New Testament Commentary (Grand Rapids: Wm. B. Eerdmans Publishing Co., 2016), 382.

[23] Aune, *Word Biblical Commentary,* 1187.

[24] Cotton, "Wonderful—God's Name," in *Wonders and the Word,* 24.

manifestations from the parameter of His salvific intentions would be to reduce Him to a 'showman' wanting only to amaze people. This, I believe, does not glorify who God truly is.

Question 4. Because of a lack of biblical precedent, weak exegetical support, and non-conformity to God's nature and message, the manifestation of gold dust can be considered as non-conforming to scriptural teaching. As discussed, the manifestation of gold dust doesn't conform to how God supernaturally intervenes in Scripture, doesn't point to the Lordship of Jesus and the salvation message of the cross, and doesn't occur anywhere else in Scripture. What it does points to are a possibility of a golden-paved heaven (having weak exegetical support) and a God who acts like a showman wanting to wow His people with glittery dust.

Synthesis

Based on the qualitative evaluation above using the four questions on biblical rootedness, one can safely conclude that the manifestation of gold dust is a phenomenon that is most probably not rooted in Scripture. Figure 3 illustrates this contention.

Figure 3. Qualitative Scale of Biblical Rootedness.

Scale of Biblical Rootedness

Gold Dust

Yes	Maybe	No
0	0	4

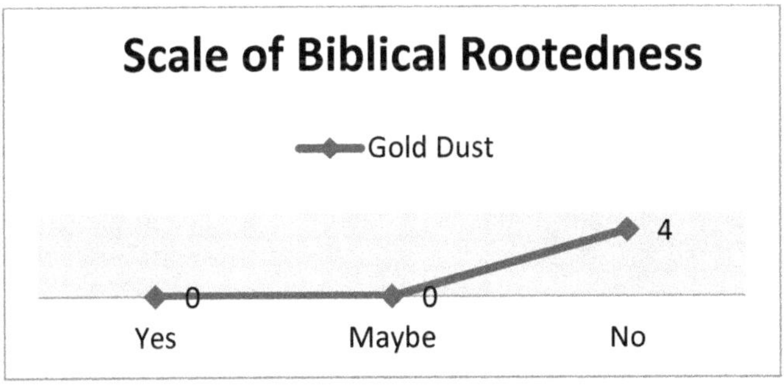

Although this evaluation does not deny the possibility of a gold dust occurrence, it does deny its biblical rootedness. Therefore, it must be classed as a 'sub-biblical phenomenon' that may occur in a revivalism setting but cannot be normatively considered manifestation of signs and wonders coming from God. Rather, it may simply be a supernatural phenomenon (source unknown), with a capability to decentralize the message of God's salvation and replace it with a message on a glorious literal heaven.

Final Analysis

The case study on gold dust demonstrates that it is possible to qualitatively assess a phenomenon's biblical rootedness using this rating scale. There should be rationalization for each assessment, however, the rationales should be supported by Scripture and other research-based evidences.

Due to space constraints, this study will not assess the other manifestations claimed by TB revivalists as manifestations of signs and wonders. Since the case study above demonstrates how such an assessment is done, others who would desire to assess a supernatural manifestation can follow the example given.

Chapter 11

Conclusion and Recommendations

Conclusion

The findings of the study affirm the initial hypothesis that TB Revivalism's signs and wonders theology in the Filipino perspective is similar to the signs and wonders theology espoused by ministers connected to the mid-1990s North American TB Revivalism. This thesis is supported by three qualitative findings.

First, the review of related literature shows the historical rootedness of this stream of revivalism to North American TB Revivalism, which was a transmutation of the P/C Movement, beginning with Pentecostalism then to the Latter Rain Movement. Although the Latter Rain Movement was debunked by Classical Pentecostals like the US Assemblies of God, part of the former's theology was picked up and expanded by Neo-Charismatics, such as John Wimber.

Wimber's 'power theology' espoused a power reception apart from the spiritual crisis-experience of Spirit baptism. Unlike Classical Pentecostalism, which views Spirit baptism as the doorway to prophetic empowerment (Acts 2), Wimber and his Third Wave Movement focused on a reception of power through intense prayer, praise, and worship in renewal services. Repetitive terms used in their ministries, include 'ushering the manifest presence of God' and 'demonstrating the power of the Kingdom.' According to Pawson, this dichotomy between Spirit baptism and spiritual empowerment eventually resulted in openness to various ways in which believers can experience sensate and sometimes sub-biblical supernatural phenomena.[1]

---

[1] Pawson, "A Mixed Blessing," 84.

When the Toronto Blessing occurred in one of the Vineyard churches in the mid-1990s, this openness to experiences of sensate and sub-biblical phenomena became central to an emerging stream of revivalism, identified in this study as 'TB revivalism'. It became world-renowned because of the intensity of cathartic experiences during their services and their claims of unusual manifestations as signs and wonders, all within the parlance of revival.

Proponents of the Toronto Blessing spread their revivalist spirituality to different parts of the world through the use of literature, the internet, media, and itinerant ministries. By the first decade of the millennium, several ministers in the Philippines were exposed to and influenced by this revivalist spirituality. Some of these ministers, such as Pangilinan and Yadao, even began participating in North American conferences organized by revivalists connected to the TB.

Today, Filipino revivalists (including the ones featured in this study) are connected to North American Revivalist networks like Che Ahn's Harvest International Ministry, Randy Clark's Apostolic Network of Global Awakening, Leif Hetland's Global Missions Awareness, and Heidi and Rolland Baker's IRIS Ministries. Some also participate in international conferences by the Revival Alliance, an alliance of North American revivalists who were impacted by the TB and who uphold the same theology of signs and wonders.

Second, Filipino TB revivalists and North American TB revivalists share the same interrelating themes in their signs and wonders theologies. Based on the findings, five such interrelating themes on signs and wonders emerged—(1) the manifest presence of God, (2) the infinite creativity of God, (3) a literal/materialized heaven, (4) the reified power of God, and (5) the divine love of God. All five are found in the signs and wonders theologies of both North American and Filipino TB revivalists. Thus, their theologies are thematically similar.

Third, both theologies consider sub-biblical supernatural phenomena as normative manifestations of signs and wonders. Promotion of the infinite creativity of God (the limitlessness of manifestations of signs and wonders) resulted in the normative treatment of sub-biblical experiences. Examples of these experiences include manifestation of gold dust, gold teeth, orbs, gemstones, angel feathers, supernatural fragrance, supernatural oil, instant height increase, instant weight change, instant hair growth, etc. These manifestations are sometimes called 'extraordinary (unusual) signs and wonders or 'glory manifestations'. Although without biblical precedent, TB revivalists claim their validity based on testimonies.

The normative treatment of these sub-biblical supernatural phenomena is considered precarious, especially in light of a split-level Christianity in the Philippines. Overemphasis of supernatural phenomena may result in the pitfalls of syncretism, magical mentality, human-centeredness, experience-based theology, theological imbalance, false guilt, and the like. As a way forward, this study strongly suggests that ministers of TB Revivalism operate within a disciplined, albeit Pentecostal, framework, where the Bible is used as the criterion for evaluating supernatural phenomena and where sub-biblical experiences are recognized but not promoted as normative.

In summary, TB Revivalism's signs and wonders theology in the Filipino perspective is a theology of reified power. It is thematically similar to that of North American TB Revivalism because Filipino TB revivalists have been influenced by North American TB revivalists. Both share the same interrelating themes and both accept sub-biblical supernatural phenomena as normative manifestations of signs and wonders. This theology has both positive and precarious implications for Filipinos in the P/C movement.

Recommendations for Further Study

There is a lacuna in the literature available concerning this narrow stream of revivalism in the Filipino P/C perspective. No academic literature has been written to discuss the emerging Neo-Charismatic Movement in the Philippines, including that connected to TB Revivalism. AJPS' two-part study on Hiram Pangilinan is the only academic literature that describes revivalism's signs and wonders theology through the lens of a Filipino TB revivalist. To gain proper understanding of this movement, more research on the Filipino Neo-Charismatic Movement and TB Revivalism ministries should be conducted.

One way to do this would be to supplement the current research with a quantitative study on the current ministries under the Neo-Charismatic Movement, specifically those who espouse the same spirituality as that of TB revivalists. The current statistical information on P/C churches is not updated, and the increasing numbers of Neo-Charismatic TB revivalists in the country are not recorded.

Lastly, a more comprehensive theological analysis of this movement's signs and wonders theology should be conducted, as this study only skimmed the surface. A thorough evaluation of their theological bases would aid in not only understanding this revivalist spirituality, but also in formulating a theological framework for discerning manifestations of signs and wonders in the P/C tradition. Using the qualitative rating scale in Chapter 10 for assessing each of the manifestation they accept as normative signs and wonders would also be recommendable in determining the biblical rootedness of their theological claims.

References Cited

Ahn, Che. *Into the Fire: How You Can Enter Renewal and Catch God's Holy Fire*. Venture, CA: Renew Books, 1998.

Aigbe, Sunday. "Pentecostal Mission and Tribal People Groups." In *Called and Empowered: Global Mission in Pentecostal Perspective*, edited by Murray A. Dempster, Byron D. Klaus, and Douglas Petersen, 165-179. Peabody, MA: Hendrickson Publishers, Inc., 1991.

Aker, Benny. "The Gospel in Action." In *Signs & Wonders in Ministry Today*, edited by Benny Aker and Gary B. McGee, 34-36. Springfield, MO: Gospel Publishing House, 1996.

Aker, Benny and Gary B. McGee, eds. *Signs & Wonders in Ministry Today*. Springfield, MO: Gospel Publishing House, 1996.

Anderson, Allan. *An Introduction to Pentecostalism*, 2nd ed. Cambridge: Cambridge University Press, 2014.

Anderson, Allan and Edmond Tang eds. *Asian and Pentecostal: The Charismatic Face of Christianity in Asia*, Revised Ed. Eugene, OR: Wipf and Stock Publishers, 2011.

Anderson, Neil T. *The Bondage Breaker*, Revised and Expanded. Eugene, OR: Harvest House Publishers, 2019.

Annacondia, Carlos. "Power Evangelism, Argentine Style." In *The Rising Revival: Firsthand Accounts of the Incredible Argentine Revival—and How It Can Spread Throughout the World*, edited by C. Peter Wagner and Pablo Deiros, 57-74. Ventura, California: Renew Books, 1998.

_____. *Listen to Me, Satan!: Exercising Authority over the Devil in Jesus Name.*, translated by Gisela Sawin and Sylvia Cudich. Lake Mary, FL: Charisma House, 1997.

Arnott, John. *The Father's Blessing*. Orlando, FL: Creation House, 1995.

Arnott, John and Carol Arnott. *Preparing for the Glory: Getting Ready for the Next Wave of Holy Spirit Outpouring*. Shippensburg, PA: Destiny Image Publishers, Inc., 2018. Kindle.

Barrett, David B. "The Worldwide Holy Spirit Renewal" In *A Century of the Holy Spirit: 100 Years of Pentecostal and Charismatic*

Renewal, edited by Vinson Synan. Nashville, TN: Thomas Nelson, 2001.

Bautista, Purificacion G. "The Cursillo Movement: Its Impact on Philippine Society." *Asian Studies* 10, no 2 (August 1972): 232-244.

Bebbington, David W. "What is Revivalism?" *Christianity Today* 25, 1990. https://www.christianitytoday.com/history/issues/issue-25/what-isrevivalism.html (accessed January 26, 2019).

_____. *Evangelicalism in Modern Britain: A History from the 1730s to the 1930s.* London: Unwin Hyman, 1989.

Benavidez, Doreen Alcoran. "The Early Years of the Church of God in Northern Luzon (19471953): A Historical and Theological Overview." *Asian Journal of Pentecostal Studies* 8, no.2 (2005): 255-269.

Beverley, James. "Vineyard Severs Ties with 'Toronto Blessing' Church." *Christianity Today* 40, no. 1 (January 8, 1996): 66.

Brown, Arthur Judson. *The New Era in the Philippines.* New York: F.H. Revell Company, 1903.

Bulatao, Jaime C. "Split-Level Christianity." *Philippine Sociological Review* XIII, no. 2 (April 1965): 119-121.

Burgess, Stanley. "Neocharismatics." In *The New International Dictionary of Pentecostal and Charismatic Movements,* revised and expanded, edited by Stanley Burgess and Eduard Van der Maas, 928. Grand Rapids, MI: Zondervan Publishing House, 2002.

Burgess, Stanley and Eduard Van der Maas eds., *The New International Dictionary of Pentecostal and Charismatic Movements.* Revised and Expanded. Grand Rapids, MI: Zondervan Publishing House, 2002.

Burgess, Stanley and Gary McGee. "Signs and Wonders." In *The New International Dictionary of Pentecostal and Charismatic Movements,* revised and expanded, edited by Stanley Burgess and Eduard Van der Maas, 1063. Grand Rapids, MI: Zondervan Publishing House, 2002.

Cartledge, Mark. "'Catch the Fire': Revivalist Spirituality from Toronto to Beyond," *PentecoStudies* 13, no. 2 (2014): 217-238.

_____. *Encountering the Spirit: The Charismatic Tradition.* London, Darton: Longmann and Todd, 2006.

Cerullo, Morris. *Victory Miracle Living: It's Harvest Time.* San Diego, CA: Morris Cerrulo Evangelism, 1982.

Chevreau, Guy. *Catch the Fire*, Reprint. Toronto, Canada: HarperCollins Publishers, 1995.

Coggins, James R. and Paul G. Hiebert, eds. *Wonders and the Word: An Examination of Issues Raised by John Wimber and the Vineyard Movement.* Winnipeg, MB, Canada: Kindred Press, 1989.

Cotton, Roger D. ""Wonderful"—God's Name." In *Signs & Wonders in Ministry Today,* edited by Benny C. Aker and Gary B. McGee, 21-33. Springfield, MO: Gospel Publishing House, 1996.

Covar, Propsero. "Pagkatao at Paniniwala (Humanity and Faith)." In *Reading Popular Culture,* edited by Soledad Reyes. Quezon City, Philippines: Ateneo de Manila, Office of Research and Publication, 1991.

Cox, Harvey. *Fire From Heaven: The Rise of Pentecostal Spirituality and the Reshaping of Christianity in the Twenty-First Century.* New York: Addison-Wesley, 2001.

Creswell, John W. *Research Design: Qualitative, Quantitative, and Mixed Methods Approaches,* 4th edition. London, UK: Sage Publications, Inc. 2014.

Davie, Martin. "A Real But Limited Renewal." In *"Toronto" in Perspective: Papers on the New Charismatic Wave of the Mid 1990s,* edited by David Hilborn, 35-44. Carlisle, UK: Paternoster Publishing, 2001.

Deck, Allan Figueroa. "Where the Laity Flourish" *America: The Jesuit Review* 195, no. 4 (August 2006). https://www.america-magazine.org/issue/580/article/where-laityflourish (accessed March 6, 2018).

Dempster, Murray A., Byron D. Klaus, and Douglas Petersen, eds. *Called and Empowered: Global Mission in Pentecostal Perspective.* Peabody, MA: Hendrickson Publishers, Inc., 1991.

Dixon, Patrick. "An Altered Christian Consciousness." In *"Toronto" in Perspective:Papers on the New Charismatic Wave of the Mid 1990s,* edited by David Hilborn, 88-98. Carlise, UK: Paternoster Press, 2001.

Duin, Julia. "An Evening with Rodney Howard-Browne." *Christian Research Journal* 17, no. 3 (1995): 43-47.

Engcoy, Dynnice Rosanny D. *Pentecostal Pioneer: The Life and Legacy of Rudy Esperanza in the Early Years of the Assemblies of God in the Philippines*. Baguio, Philippines: APTS Press, 2013.

_____. "A Reflection of a Missionary to the Philippines: Gary A. Denbow Interview." *Asian Journal of Pentecostal Studies* 8, no. 2 (2005): 311-330.

Esperanza, Trinidad C. "The Assemblies of God in the Philippines." Ph.D. Dissertation. Fuller Theological Seminary, USA, 1965.

Geisler, Norman. *Signs and Wonders*. Wheaton, IL: Tyndale House Publishers, Inc., 1988.

Geivett, Douglas and Holly Pivec. *A New Apostolic Reformation: A Biblical Response to a Worldwide Movement*. Wooster, OH: Weaver Book Company, 2014.

Gener, Timoteo. "Evangelicals and Catholics Together? Issues and Prospects for Dialogue and Common Witness in Lowland Philippines." *Evangelical Review of Theology*, 33, no. 3 (2009): 228-245.

Glasser, Art. "The Miraculous in Ministry." In *Wonders and the Word: An Examination of Issues Raised by John Wimber and the Vineyard Movement,* edited by James R. Coggins and Paul G. Hiebert, 98-108. Winnipeg, Canada: Kindred Press, 1989.

Gohr, G. W. "Hinn, Benedictus (Benny)." In *The New International Dictionary of Pentecostal and Charismatic Movements*, Revised and Expanded, edited by Stanley Burgess and Eduard Van der Maas, 714-715. Grand Rapids, MI: Zondervan, 2003.

Gonzales, Arthur V. "Inner Healing from Deep Wounds." In *Signs and Wonders,* edited by Dante Veluz, 165-205. Quezon City, Philippines: Jesus, the Heart of Missions Team, Inc., 1999.

Hannah, John. "Jonathan Edwards, The Toronto Blessing, and the Spiritual Gifts: Are the Extraordinary Ones Actually the Ordinary Ones?" *Trinity Journal* 17, no. 2 (1996): 167-189.

Hawtin, George R. "Latter Rain Movement, 'Letter to Wayne Warner." In *Pentecostal and Charismatic: A Reader,* edited by William K. Kay and Anne E. Dyer, 19-21. London: SCM Press, 1987.

Heflin, Ruth Ward. *Glory: Experiencing the Atmosphere of Heaven*. Hagerstown, MD: McDougal Publishing, 1990.

Henry, Rodney L. *Filipino Spirit World: A Challenge to the Church.* Manila: OMF Literature, 1986.

Hetland, Leif and Paul Yadao. *The Ultimate Transformation* (Peachtree, GA: Global Missions Awareness, 2015.

Hiebert, Paul G. "Healing and the Kingdom." In *Wonders and the Word: An Examination of Issues Raised by John Wimber and the Vineyard Movement,* edited by James R. Coggins and Paul G. Hiebert, 109-152. Winnipeg, Canada: Kindred Press, 1989.

Hiebert, Paul G., R. Daniel Shaw, and Tite Tiénou. *Understanding Folk Religion: A Christian Response to Popular Beliefs and Practices.* Grand Rapids, MI: Baker Books, 1999.

Hilborn, David ed. *"Toronto" in Perspective: Papers on the New Charismatic Wave of Mid-1990s.* Carlisle, UK: Paternoster Press, 2001.

_____. "Introduction: Evangelicalism, the Evangelical Alliance and the Toronto Blessing." In *"Toronto" in Perspective: Papers on the New Charismatic Wave of the Mid 1990s,* edited by David Hilborn, 3-34. Carlisle, UK: Paternoster Publishing, 2001.

_____. "Part II: A Chronicle of the Toronto Blessing." In *"Toronto" in Perspective: Papers on the New Charismatic Wave of the Mid 1990s,* edited by David Hilborn, 131-151. Carlisle, UK: Paternoster Publishing, 2001.

_____. "The Rise of the Blessing." In *"Toronto" in Perspective: Papers on the New Charismatic Wave of the Mid 1990s,* edited by David Hilborn, 152-210. Carlisle, UK: Paternoster Publishing, 2001.

_____. "The Spread and Critique of the Blessing." In *"Toronto" in Perspective: Papers on the New Charismatic Wave of the Mid 1990s,* edited by David Hilborn, 211-286. Carlisle, UK: Paternoster Publishing, 2001.

Hislop, Stephen K. "Anitism: A Survey of Religious Beliefs Native to the Philippines." *Asian Studies* 9, no. 2 (1971): 144-156.

Hunt, Stephen. "Charismatic Revival and Precarious Charisma: The Florida Healing 'Outpouring'." *Journal for the Academic Study of Religion* 22, no. 1 (2009): 83-108.

_____. "The 'Toronto Blessing': A Rumour of Angels?" *Journal of Contemporary Religion* 10, no. 3 (October 1995): 83-108.

Hunter, Charles and Frances Hunter. *Handbook for Healing,* Revised. New Kensington, PA: Whitaker House, 2001.

Jackson, Bill. *The Quest for the Radical Middle: A History of the Vineyard.* Capetown, South Africa: Vineyard International Publishing, 2010. Kindle.

Jocano, F. Landa. *Filipino Worldview: Ethnography of Local Knowledge*, Anthropology of the Filipino People V. Metro Manila, Philippines: PUNLAD Research House Inc., 2001.

_____. *Folk Christianity: A Preliminary Study of Conversion and Patterning of Christian Experiences in the Philippines,* Monograph Series 1. Quezon City, Philippines: Trinity Research Institute, 1981.

Jong, Yong Jeong. "Filipino Pentecostal Spirituality: An Investigation into Filipino Indigenous Spirituality and Pentecostalism in the Philippines." Ph.D. Dissertation. University of Birmingham, 2001.

Johnson, Bill. *The Supernatural Power of a Transformed Mind: Access to a Life of Miracles.* Shippensburg, PA: Destiny Image Publishers, Inc., 2005.

Johnson, Dave. *Theology in Context: A Case Study in the Philippines.* Baguio, Philippines: APTS Press, 2013.

_____. *Led by the Spirit: The History of the American Assemblies of God in the Philippines.* Pasig City, Philippines: ICI Ministries, Inc., 2009.

Johnson, Todd. "The Demographics of Renewal." In *Spirit-Empowered Christianity in the Twenty-First Century: Insights, Analysis, and Future Trends from World Renowned Scholars*, edited by Vinson Synan, 55-68. Lake Mary, FL: Charisma House, 2011.

Joyner, Rick. *The Final Quest.* New Kensington, PA: Whitaker House, 1996.

Kim, (Elijah) Jong Fil. "Contemporary Pentecostal Charismatic Movements: On a Double Structured Religious System in Greater Metro Manila." Ph.D. Dissertation, University of Birmingham, UK, 2004.

King, Johnny Loye. "Spirit and Schism: A History of Oneness Pentecostalism in the Philippines." Ph.D. Dissertation. Birmingham University, UK, 2017. http://etheses.bham.ac.uk (accessed April 14, 2019).

Kroeber, A. L. *Peoples of the Philippines*. New York: American Museum of Natural History, 1928.

Kydd, Ronald. "A Retrospectus/Prospectus on Physical Phenomena Centered on the 'Toronto Blessing.'" *Journal of Pentecostal Theology* 6, no. 12 (1998): 73-81.

Ladd, George Eldon. *Theology of the New Testament,* Revised. Grand Rapids, MI: Wm. B. Eerdmans Publishing Co., 1993.

Lambert, Vickie and Clinton Lambert, "Qualitative Descriptive Research: An Acceptable Design." *Pacific Rim International Journal of Nursing Research* 16, no. 4 (December 2012): 255-256. https://www.tcithaijo.org/index.php/PRIJNR/article/ view/5805 (accessed May 12, 2018).

Latham, Steve. "'God Came From Teman': Revival and Contemporary Revivalism." In *On Revival: A Critical Examination*, edited by Andrew Walker and Kristine Aune, 171-186. Carlisle, UK: Paternoster Press, 2003.

Lim, David S. "Indigenous Mission Movement of the Philippines." Accessed March 16,2019.https://www.academia.edu/12304593/ Philippine_Misions_Mobilization_Movement.

Lumahan, Conrado. "Facts and Figures: A History of the Growth of the Philippine Assemblies of God." *Asian Journal of Pentecostal Studies* 8, no. 2 (2005): 331-344.

Lyons, John. "The Fourth Wave and the Approaching Millennium: Some Problems with Charismatic Movements." *Anvil* 15, no. 3 (1998): 169-180.

Ma, Julie. *When the Spirit Meets the Spirits: Pentecostal Ministry among the Kankana-ey Tribe in the Philippines.* Studies in the Intercultural/History of Christianity, 111. Frankfurt am Main: Peter Lang, 2000.

Ma, Wonsuk. "Doing Theology in the Philippines: A Case of Pentecostal Christianity." *Asian Journal of Pentecostal Studies* 8, no. 2 (2005): 215-233.

_____. "Philippines." in *The New International Dictionary of Pentecostal and Charismatic Movements*, Revised and Expanded, edited by Stanley Burgess and Eduard Van der Maas, 201. Grand Rapids, MI: Zondervan, 2003.

_____. "A 'First Waver' Looks at the 'Third Wave': A Pentecostal Reflection on Charles Kraft's Power Encounter Terminology." *Pneuma* 19, no. 2 (Fall 1997):189-206.

Martin, David. *Pentecostalism: The World Their Parish*. Oxford, UK: Blackwell Publishers, 2002.

McGee, Gary and B. A. Pavia. "Wagner, Charles Peter." In *The New International Dictionary of Pentecostal and Charismatic Movements*, Revised and Expanded, edited by Stanley Burgess and Eduard Van der Maas, 1181. Grand Rapids, MI: Zondervan, 2003.

McLoughlin, William Gerald. *Modern Revivalism: Charles Grandison Finney to Billy Graham*. New York: Ronald Press, 1959.

Melton, J. Gordon and Martin Baumann, eds. *Religions of the World: A Comprehensive Encyclopedia of Beliefs and Practices,* 2nd edition. Sta. Barbara, CA: ABC-CLIO, LLC, 2010.

Melton, J. Gordon and Clifton Holland. "Argentina" in *Religions of the World: A Comprehensive Encyclopedia of Beliefs and Practices,* 2nd edition, edited by J. Gordon Melton and Martin Baumann, 168-178. Sta. Barbara, CA: ABC-CLIO, LLC., 2010.

Menzies, Robert P. *Pentecost: This Story Is Our Story*. Springfield, MO: Gospel Publishing House, 2013.

Mercado, Leonardo. *Inculturation and Filipino Theology,* Asia Pacific Theological Series. Techny, IL: Divine Word Publications, 1992.

_____. *Christ in the Philippines*. Tacloban, Philippines: Divine Word Publications, 1982.

Murray, Iain. *Revival and Revivalism: The Making and Marring of Evangelical Revivalism 1750-1858.* Carlisle, PA: Banner of Truth, 1994.

Nathan, Rich and Ken Wilson. *Empowered Evangelicals: Bringing Together the Best of the Evangelical and Charismatic Worlds.* Ann Arbor, MI: Servant Publications, 1995.

Oconer, Luther Jeremiah. "The Manila Healing Revival and the First Pentecostal Defections in the Methodist Church in the Philippines." *Pneuma: The Journal of the Society of Pentecostal Studies* 31, no.1 (March 2009): 66-84.

Pangilinan, Hiram. *Presence Driven: The Blessings of Hungering for God's Presence*. Quezon City, Philippines: HG Pangilinan Books Marketing, 2016.

———. *Handbook on Deliverance*, Expanded. Quezon City, Philippines: HG Pangilinan Books Marketing, 2016.

———. *Healing is Yours*. Quezon City, Philippines: HG Pangilinan Books, Marketing, 2016.

———. *Be Healed: A Primer on Healing*. Quezon City, Philippines: HG Pangilinan Books Marketing, 2015.

———. *Sorry Po: Releasing the Power of Forgiveness*. Quezon City, Philippines: HG Pangilinan Books Marketing, 2015.

———. *Discovering Jesus,* Revised. Quezon City, Philippines: HG Pangilinan Books Marketing, 2015.

———. *Miracle Money*. Quezon City, Philippines: HG Pangilinan Books Marketing, 2015.

———. *What if God Comes?* Quezon City, Philippines: Revival Publishing, 2011.

———. *Hula, Multo, Faith Healing, Atbp.: Exposé ng Occult Sa Pilipinas*. Manila, Philippines: OMF Literature, 2010.

———. "Spiritual Warfare Foundations." In *Signs and Wonders*, edited by Dante Veluz. Quezon City, Philippines: Jesus, the Heart of Missions Team, Inc., 1999.

Pawson, David. "A Mixed Blessing." In *"Toronto" in Perspective: Papers on the New Charismatic Wave of the Mid 1990s*, edited by David Hilborn, 75-87. Carlisle, UK: Paternoster Publishing, 2001.

Percy, Martyn. "Adventure and Atrophy in a Charismatic Movement: Returning to 'Toronto Blessing'." *Journal of Contemporary Religion* 20, no.1 (2005): 71-90.

Phillips, Tom. *Revival Signs: Join the New Spiritual Awakening*. Gresham, OR: Vision House Publishing, Inc. 1995.

Poloma, Margaret. "Toronto Blessing." In *The New International Dictionary of Pentecostal and Charismatic Movement,* Revised and Expanded, edited by Stanley Burgess and Eduard Van der Maas. 1149. Grand Rapids, Michigan: Zondervan, 2003.

———. *Main Street Mystics: The Toronto Blessing and Reviving Pentecostalism*. Walnut Creek, CA: Alta Mira Press, 2003.

———. "A Reconfiguration of Pentecostalism." In *"Toronto in Perspective: Papers on the New Charismatic Wave of the Mid 1990s,* edited by David Hilborn, 99-127. Carlise, UK: Paternoster Press, 2001.

_____. "Inspecting the Fruit of the 'Toronto Blessing': A Sociological Perspective." *Pneuma: The Journal of the Society of Pentecostal Studies* 20, no.1 (Spring 1998): 43-70.

_____. "The 'Toronto Blessing': Charisma, Institutionalization, and Revival." *Journal of the Scientific Study of Religion* 36, no. 2 (June 1997): 257-271.

Rabey, Steve. "Pensacola Outpouring Keeps Gushing." *Christianity Today* 41, no. 3 (March 1997): 54, 56-57.

Rich, John A. "Religious Acculturation in the Philippines." *Practical Anthropology* 17, no. 5 (1970): 196-209.

Richter, P. J. "'God Is Not a Gentleman!': The Sociology of the Toronto Blessing." In *The Toronto Blessing or Is It?* edited by S.E. Porter and P.J. Richter, 5-37. London, Darton: Longman and Todd, 1995.

Riss, Richard. "A History of the Awakening 1992-1995." In *The Revival Library,* chap. 2. http://www.revival-library.org/index.php/cataloguesmenu/ pentecostal/a-history-of-the-awakening-of-1992-1995 (accessed February 21, 2019).

_____. "The Latter Rain Movement of 1948." *Pneuma* 4, no. 1 (Spring 1982): 32-45.

Santiago, Radziwill. "Exposing the Deeds of Darkness." In *Signs and Wonders,* edited by Dante Veluz, 207-228. Quezon City, Philippines: Jesus, the Heart of Missions Team, Inc., 1999.

Smail, Tom. "The Cross and the Spirit: Toward a Theology of Renewal." In *The Love of Power,Or, the Power of Love: A Careful Assessment of the Problems Within the Charismatic and Word-of-Faith Movements,* edited by Thomas Smail and Andrew Walker, 13-35. Minneapolis, MN: Bethany House Publishers, 1994.

Smail, Tom, Andrew Walker and Nigel Wright eds. *Charismatic Renewal: The Search for a Theology.* London: Society for Promoting Christian Knowledge, 1995.

Smith, Richard J. "A Consideration of the Toronto Blessing." *Didaskalia* 11, no. 1 (Fall 1999):15-30.

Smith, Sam. *Miracles in Moroland: A Journey of Faith, Love & Courage—The Inside Story of the Sipadan Hostage Crises.* Quezon City, Philippines: Jesus Miracle Crusade International Ministry, 2015.

Stafford, Tim. "Miracles in Mozambique: How Mama Heidi Reaches the Abandoned." *Christianity Today* 56, no.5 (May 2012): 18. https://www.christianitytoday.com/ct/ 2012/may/miracles-in-mozambique.html (accessed February 23, 2018).

Stibbe, Mark. *Times of Refreshing: A Practical Theology of Revival.* London: Marshall Pickering, 1995.

Strom, Andrew. *Kundalini Warning: Are False Spirits Invading the Church?* RevivalSchool, 2015. E-book.

Suico, Joseph ed. "Philippines Pentecostalism." *Asian Journal of Pentecostal Studies* 8, no. 2 (2005).

Sumrall, Lester. *The Story of Clarita Villanueva: A Seventeen Year Old Girl Bitten by Devils in Bilibid Prison, Manila, Philippines.* Manila: Lester F. Sumrall, 1955.

_____. *Modern Manila Miracles.* Springfield, MO: Rev. Clifton E. Erickson, 1954.

Synan, Vinson. ed. *Spirit-Empowered Christianity in the Twenty-First Century: Insights, Analysis, and Future Trends from World-Renowned Scholars.* Lake Mary, FL: Charisma House, 2011.

_____. "Classical Pentecostalism." In *The New International Dictionary of Pentecostal and Charismatic Movement,* Revised and Expanded, edited by Stanley Burgess and Eduard Van der Maas, 553. Grand Rapids, MI: Zondervan, 2003.

_____ ed. *The Century of the Holy Spirit: 100 Years of Pentecostal and Charismatic Renewal 1901-2001.* Nashville, TN: Thomas Nelson, 2001.

_____. *In The Latter Days: The Outpouring of the Holy Spirit in the Twentieth Century,* Revised. Ann Arbor, MI: Servant Publications, 1991.

Tappeiner, Daniel A. *The Mantle of Philip: Practical Steps to a Ministry of Signs and Wonders.* Makati, Philippines: Life Schools Ministry, 1997.

Toliver, Ralph. "Syncretism, A Specter Among Philippine Protestants." *Practical Anthropology* 17, no. 5 (1970): 210-219.

Embudo-Timenia, Lora Angeline. "Critical Understanding of a Filipino Third Wave Signs and Wonders Theology: A Case Study of Hiram Pangilinan: Part 1." *Asian Journal of Pentecostal Studies,* 22, no.1 (2019): 31-47.

_____. "Critical Understanding of a Filipino Third Wave Signs and Wonders Theology: A Case Study of Hiram Pangilinan: Part 2." *Asian Journal of Pentecostal Studies,* 22, no.1 (2019): 49-63.

Tuggy, Arthur. *The Philippine Church: Growth in a Changing Society.* Grand Rapids, MI: William B. Eerdmans Publishing Co., 1971.

Veluz, Dante ed. *Signs and Wonders.* Philippines: Jesus, the Heart of Missions Team,1999.

Wagner, C. Peter and Pablo Deiros eds. *The New Apostolic Churches: Rediscovering the New Testament Model of Leadership and Why It's God's Desire for the Church Today.* Ada, MI: Baker Publishing Group, 2000.

_____. *The Rising Revival: Firsthand Accounts of the Incredible Argentine Revival—and How It Can Spread Throughout the World.* Venture, CA: Renew Books, 1998.

_____. *Confronting the Powers: How the New Testament Church Experienced the Power of Strategic-Level Spiritual Warfare*, The Prayer Warrior Series. Ventura, CA: Regal Books, 1991.

Ware, S. L. "Restorationism in Classical Pentecostalism." In *The New International Dictionary of Pentecostal and Charismatic Movements*, Revised and Expanded, edited by Stanley Burgess and Eduard Van der Maas, 1020-1021. Grand Rapids, MI: Zondervan, 2003.

Wiegele, Katharine Leone. "Transforming Popular Catholicism: The El Shaddai Movement of the Philippines." Ph.D. Dissertation, University of Illinois, 2002.

Wilson, D. J. "Kuhlman, Kathryn." In *The New International Dictionary of Pentecostal Studies,* Revised and Expanded, edited by Stanley Burgess and Eduard Van der Maas, 826-827. Grand Rapids, MI: Zondervan, 2003.

Wostyn, Lode. "Catholic Charismatics in the Philippines." In *Asian and Pentecostal: The Charismatic Face of Christianity in Asia,* Regnum Studies in Mission: Asian Journal of Pentecostal Studies 3, edited by Allan Anderson and Edmond Tang, 294-328. Oxford, UK: Regnum Books International, 2005; Baguio, Philippines: APTS Press, 2005.

Wright, Nigel. "The Theology and Methodology of 'Signs and Wonders.'" In *Charismatic Renewal: Search for a Theology*, edited by Tom Smail, Andrew Walker and Nigel Wright, 37-52. London: Society for Promoting Christian Knowledge, 1995.

_____. "Theology of Signs and Wonders." In *The Love of Power, Or, the Power of Love,* edited by Tom Smail and Andrew Walker, 37-52. London: Bethany House Publishers, 1994.

Yadao, Paul. *The Mark.* Laguna, Philippines: Destiny Ministries International, 2011.

Yadao, Paul and Leif Hetland. *Soaking in God's Presence.* (Peach tree, GA: Global Missions Awareness, 2013.

Yung, Hwa. "Pentecostalism and the Asian Church." In *Asian and Pentecostal: The Charismatic Face of Christianity in Asia,* revised ed., edited by Allan Anderson and Edmond Tang, 37-57. Eugene, OR: Wipf and Stock Publishers, 2011.

www.ingramcontent.com/pod-product-compliance
Lightning Source LLC
Chambersburg PA
CBHW051930160426
43198CB00012B/2100